PRACTICAL
FALCONRY

Other books by James McKay and published by Quiller

The Complete Jack Russell
Complete Guide to Ferrets
Ferret Breeding

PRACTICAL
FALCONRY

James McKay

Quiller

First published in the UK in 2010
by Quiller, an imprint of Quiller Publishing Ltd

British Library Cataloguing-in-Publication Data
A catalogue record for this book is available from the British Library.

ISBN 978 1 84689 029 1

Book and jacket design by Sharyn Troughton
Title page photograph by Nick Ridley

Printed in China

Quiller

An imprint of Quiller Publishing Ltd
Wykey House, Wykey, Shrewsbury, SY4 1JA
Tel: 01939 261616 Fax: 01939 261606
E-mail: info@quillerbooks.com
Website: www.countrybooksdirect.com

CONTENTS

INTRODUCTION

Birds of prey and owls, collectively known as raptors, hold a fascination for many people. For some, simply being able to occasionally see these magnificent birds is all that they ask; for others it becomes an overriding passion. For a few, raptors become a way of life, and for an even smaller number of people, they become a living. I consider myself extremely lucky that, today, I make my living by working with raptors.

Along with my wife and son, I run the UK's National Falconry School, based in Derbyshire, and spend my working hours with eagles, hawks, buzzards, falcons and owls. The work is varied – hunting with the birds (hawking); teaching newcomers the sport of falconry; giving the man in the street the opportunity to sample the sport without any commitment; giving public displays; visiting schools, colleges and universities; training police wildlife crime officers and veterinary professionals; and supplying raptors for use in TV and film productions. Every day brings new challenges and excitement, and over the years I have made many great friends – I wouldn't change it for the world.

In this book, I have attempted to distil some of the knowledge I have gained over the many years in which I have been a practising falconer. During those years, I have been privileged to hawk with many extremely experienced falconers, and have learned much from them. I have also learned much from the birds themselves.

Likewise, this book will also look at, explain and advise on different breeding methods such as artificial insemination, artificial incubation, imprinting, parent-reared and creche-reared clutches, giving both the positives and the negatives of all methods.

As with the production of any publication, this book owes a lot to the people who have helped and encouraged me, and given me the benefit of their wisdom, skill and knowledge, as well as help, assistance, guidance and support. In particular, I thank my wife, Jane, and my son, Tom, who have both been pillars of strength to me, always having an encouraging word and never being negative about my efforts and plans. My son has helped immensely with the photography for this book, in ideas, as a photographer and as a model. My wife has always been there to ensure that we are both looked after, chivvied along when necessary and encouraged. This book has seen more teamwork from the McKay family, and long may it continue. Thank you both, for everything.

I must also thank a good friend, and veterinary surgeon, Ryan James, MRCVS. Ryan has painstakingly read through the manuscript for this volume, and happily recommended amendments and alterations. Thank you for your help and support.

While I am pleased to acknowledge the increasing number of female falconers taking part in our sport, purely for the sake of simplicity, 'the falconer' is referred to throughout the text as 'he'.

I hope that there aren't too many mistakes within the pages of this book, but if there are, they are mine, and mine alone.

James McKay
Director
The National Falconry School
Derbyshire

CHAPTER 1

A BRIEF HISTORY OF FALCONRY

Falconry, or hawking, is an old sport but, for some reason, some practitioners seem to feel the need to exaggerate its age, rather like the sad anglers who exaggerate the size of their catch. I have heard falconers claim that the sport is over 15,000 years old – a ridiculous claim that can in no way be substantiated. To make such claims does falconry a grave injustice.

One of the factors which can lead to confusion regarding the date when falconry began is that hawks, along with many other species of animals, were (indeed still are) kept in captivity for many reasons other than falconry. It is still the practice today to give rare and/or impressive species to visiting dignitaries: examples of this include the gift of two giant pandas (Ching-Ching and Chia-Chia) to the then UK Prime Minister, Ted Heath, in 1974, and the gift of a highly spirited and highly strung Akhal-Teke stallion to UK Prime Minister John Major by the President of Turkmenistan, in 1991. The horse, named Maksat, was worth over £30,000, but rejected for use by the UK forces as being 'too frisky'.

People will keep animals in captivity to show their apparent mastery over the species; to establish their own importance; to earn money from breeding the animals and, of course, for food.

Obviously then, some raptorial species would have been kept in captivity for many reasons, long before man trained and used them for hawking. Likewise, paintings, cave drawings or any art depicting hawks or other raptors hunting and killing animals need not necessarily refer to falconry, but may simply be depictions of natural hunting by such birds.

Also, some pictures and records of seeming falconry are, in fact, more likely to be of 'daring' for larks. This was a method of trapping larks – a gourmet delicacy – whereby a trained hobby was flown to keep the larks on the ground, while the human hunters used nets to catch them.

My own research, and that of many other falconers, has shown that *probably* the earliest account of true falconry (i.e. the use of specially trained raptorial species of bird for hunting live quarry) can be found in the Far East. Documentary evidence shows that, in AD 244, the Chinese Empress, Jingu, sent trained goshawks (*Accipiter gentilis*) to the Emperor of Japan. Unfortunately, once in Japan, the training of the goshawks appears to have ceased, and the sport vanished from that country for over one hundred years. It was in the reign of the Emperor Nintoku (*circa* AD 355), when a raptor was presented to him, that the sport got a good grip in Japan. The bird was identified as a goshawk by a Korean member of the Japanese court, and the Emperor charged the Korean with training the bird for falconry purposes. Later that year, complete with jesses and a tail bell, the goshawk was hunted in a field near Mozu (near to the modern city of Osaka), and successfully caught several pheasants. Obviously, this story indicates that falconry was already practised in Korea and China, long before it was practised in Japan.

After this success, the Japanese Emperor was hooked on falconry, and established what would today be referred to as a falconry school. That this school was highly successful and popular can be attested to by the fact that it was still in existence many hundreds of years later. About two hundred years after its establishment, a dog keeper/trainer was conferred on the school, in order to breed and train dogs to be used in falconry.

Falconry in Japan became so popular that, during medieval times, there were many reports of great damage being done to crops due to the large size of the numerous hawking parties tramping around the country after suitable game. There are also several reports from this time of serious incidents involving hawks chasing their quarry into Buddhist temples and killing their prey in front of monks who, to say the least, were extremely offended by this action. Consequently, the Emperor banned all hawking practices from the vicinity of Buddhist temples.

The Japanese were determined to keep the sport of falconry in their country, and invited falconers from other nations to visit their country, in order that they could learn more from them. One such visitor was a renowned Chinese falconer who impressed the Japanese falconers with his skill and knowledge. In order to ensure that the Chinese falconer remained in the country, the Japanese Emperor ordered a female member of his court to seduce the Chinese falconer. The couple married, and produced a daughter, Akemihikari, who also became a famous falconer. When Akemihikari married Minamo Masayori, Akemihikari's father passed on the 'secrets' of his art, and Masayori took this knowledge and tweaked it to an extent whereby the training methods became known as the Masayori Method.

From China, Japan and Korea, the sport of falconry began to spread westwards, and a bas relief (a sculptural relief that projects slightly from the background) dating from *circa* AD 500 was found in the 'Villa of the Falconer' at Argos, Greece.

Falconry was being practised in England in Saxon times, as can be evidenced by the fact that the Archbishop of Mayence, Boniface, sent a hawk and two falcons to King Aethelbald of Mercia, sometime between AD 733 and AD 750. Hawking became extremely popular in England, and similar problems regarding damaged crops arose here, too, as they had in Japan.

Chronicles from the Middle Ages inform us that both Edward the Confessor and Athelstan were keen falconers, while the world famous Bayeux Tapestry depicts several knights, as well as Harold, carrying hawks while riding on horseback. In order that knights could have some 'R&R' time between battles, hawks and hounds were regularly taken on campaign by armies of the era. When Edward III, who made the theft of a trained hawk a crime punishable by death, invaded France, he took with him thirty falconers and many hawks.

Such was the importance of the sport that part of the education of well-to-do young men of Middle Ages England involved learning the finer points of the art of falconry, which also put fresh meat on the tables of countless families. It is important to note that falconry, although a social pastime, was also a very important means of supplying fresh meat for the household. The nursery rhyme 'Four and twenty black birds' is a good illustration of this. The birds in the rhyme are not blackbirds (*Turdus merula*), but birds that are black – rooks (*Corvus frugilegus*). Rook was a staple of the medieval diet, and the best way of catching enough birds for a pie, before the advent of accurate firearms, was to have a trained bird of prey chase and catch the rooks.

Throughout the great western civilisations, falconry was a highly regarded sport, and monarchs would send and receive hawks from their neighbours: the King of Norway sent a cast of gyr falcons (*Falco rusticolus*) to King John, and Edward III was also sent hawks from that country. In 1764, the Dukes of Atholl were granted the feudal tenancy of the Isle of Man for the rent of two white gyr falcons, which were to be paid to each succeeding monarch on the day of their coronation.

The first recorded occurrence of falconry in the Americas was when Cortes, the Spanish conquistador, arrived in Mexico, and discovered that the Aztec king, Montezuma, had an establishment for hawking, maintaining many trained birds which he used for hunting.

In Tudor England, falconry continued to gain popularity, with both Henry VIII and Queen Elizabeth I being extremely keen falconers. Henry was saved from drowning by his falconer, Edmund Mundy, when the King fell into a dyke while indulging his passion for falconry at Hitchin, Hertfordshire. Richard II had earlier built the Royal Mews at Charing Cross to house his hawks (the word 'mews' derives from the French word *muer*, meaning to moult) and it was Henry VIII who turned the mews into stables following a fire which destroyed the Royal Stables in Bloomsbury. The current Royal Mews are at Buckingham Palace, and are used exclusively for stabling horses.

Queen Elizabeth I reprimanded her Royal Falconer, Sir Ralph Sadler for failing in his duties when, after being entrusted with guarding Mary, Queen of Scots, Sir Ralph took Mary (herself a keen falconer) on several hawking trips.

In England, falconry suffered a body blow to its popularity during the Commonwealth (1649–1660), when all such pastimes were frowned upon by the Puritan establishment. However, the restoration of the monarchy saw falconry once more become highly fashionable, and when the Russian Ambassador to London went to pay homage to Charles II, he took numerous hawks with him to the Royal Court, as presents for the new king, who wore a specially made hawking glove for the purpose of receiving these gifts. Falconry continued to flourish when the Dukes of St Albans were appointed as Hereditary Grand Falconers by James II, in 1688; the office endures to the present day.

Unfortunately, another body blow – or rather two such blows – awaited falconry, in the shape of new laws and new inventions. The Enclosures Acts made falconry a very difficult pastime, since it is difficult enough to get humans to recognise lines on a map, over which they cannot cross, and is obviously totally impossible to get any animals to do so. The invention which brought about a steep decline in the popularity of the sport of falconry was the accurate firearm. To be a good falconer and have good hawks, entails hard work, time, practice and not a little skill; the birds must also be cared for and maintained every day of the year. Even so, the bag at the end of a day's hawking will never be big. With guns, although some skill and time are needed, these aspects are far less important than with hawks – the bag for a good day's shoot will always exceed that for a day's hawking. Add in the fact that guns and shooting were now modern, trendy and fashionable, and it is easy to see why the sport of falconry declined.

To help maintain the sport, falconers banded together and, in 1792, the Norfolk High Ash Falconry Club was formed, with Lord Orford as its president, but the club was disbanded in 1838. In Holland, falconers formed the Loo Hawking Club, which

The author giving a display with a male Harris' Hawk. (*Photo: Nick Ridley*)

had many members of the European aristocracy in its ranks, and Prince Alexander of the Netherlands was the club's president. Unfortunately, this club established the exclusivity of falconry, having an annual subscription many times the income of most 'normal' people, and so falconry became much less accessible to the common man, and an elitist attitude grew among the privileged few.

In 1853, the English Old Hawking Club was formed, the last English club to have professional falconers and club hawks; it also had its own headquarters until the club disbanded in 1927. In the same year, the British Falconers' Club was established, consisting entirely of amateurs, who trained and flew their own hawks.

Today, there are several thousand falconers in the UK, and many more worldwide. In the UK, numbers were boosted by the introduction of the Harris' hawks (*Parabuteo unicinctus*), a bird which has become extremely popular, despite many opponents who derogate the bird by labelling it as a 'beginner's hawk'. While it is true that the Harris' does indeed make a wonderful beginner's hawk, it is also, in the right hands, capable of being a superb bird to fly at a wide range of quarry, over varying types of country. Unfortunately, the Harris' hawk has also led to many people keeping hawks who probably, with the best will in the world, would be better not doing so. Extremely expensive when first introduced into the UK, these birds have been bred intensively and haphazardly in attempts to make money for their owners. Such people tend to keep the birds in poor conditions, feed them on a very poor and inadequate diet, and generally have little thought for the long-term well-being of the birds they produce. Such breeders have driven down the price of Harris' hawks to a mere fraction of what it was twenty years ago, and thus encouraged many unsuitable people to purchase such a hawk. That this has done a grave disservice to British falconry cannot be denied.

CHAPTER 2

SUITABLE SPECIES OF HAWK

First and foremost, I must emphasise that everyone has his/her own idea about what makes the 'best' hawk – vive la difference! I must also point out that, to a falconer, *every* bird of prey which he flies is known as a hawk, regardless of the bird's zoological category: a falconer will refer to a peregrine falcon as a hawk in the same way that he would refer to a goshawk as a hawk. Add to this confusing situation the difference in terms used either side of the Atlantic, where in America a buzzard is what we Brits would call a vulture, and confusion will really set in. Just to emphasise this point, some species are being reclassified. While some of this reclassification is being carried out by taxonomists, some is being carried out by amateur (and usually unqualified) 'scientists' (please see 'The Ferruginous Buzzard', page 23).

To falconers, all birds of prey are 'classified' in accordance with certain morphological (structural) characteristics, and placed in one of three categories, viz:

- Shortwings
- Broadwings
- Longwings

It would be an impossible task to attempt to list all of the species used by falconers in just one country, let alone worldwide, and so the following merely lists the most commonly encountered species flown by British falconers. Apologies to all adherents of species omitted from this list.

SHORTWINGS

These are true hawks, members of the genus *Accipiter*. All such birds have short, stubby wings, with large tails – this combination allows them to manoeuvre between trees, branches, etc. when flying through woodland. Such species are found in woodland, forest and tracts of land bordering such country. Traditionally, all such species are flown from the fist (often out of the hood) at quarry. The smaller species are often thrown or launched at the quarry. All shortwings are brought back to the fist after their flight.

It should also be noted that accipiters are some of the most difficult birds to train and fly for falconry.

BROADWINGS

Species of the genera *Buteo* (buzzards) or *Parabuteo*, although many falconers also include the 'true' eagles (genus *Aquila*) and a few other species of eagle. The wings of species in this category are long and broad, and most species have a very large tail. Such hawks are brought back to the fist, a dummy bunny or sometimes a swung lure.

A falconer who flies only broadwings and/or shortwings is known as an austringer, although this term is rarely used today; rather, the generic term of falconer is used.

LONGWINGS

A bird of the genus *Falco*, i.e. what zoologists term falcons. Species within this category have long, scythe-shaped wings and are flown in open country, being brought back to the handler via the swung lure.

SHORTWINGS

THE SPARROWHAWK (*Accipiter nisus*)

Arguably one of, if not *the*, most difficult of all birds to train and fly for falconry purposes, the sparrowhawk is tiny, feisty and temperamental. In her book *Falconry – Art and Practice*, Emma Ford describes these birds as being 'hysterical little hawks' – a well-founded description. In many ways, this species closely resembles its large cousin, the goshawk, which is also a fairly difficult bird to train and fly for falconry purposes, and neither species should be attempted by beginners, or indeed any falconer who has not had several years' experience with other species. Even then, the sparrowhawk should not be attempted until the austringer has trained and flown at least one goshawk, as considerable expertise and experience is needed for this species.

While some falconers may feel that an austringer with some experience will be able to make a half-decent job of training a female sparrowhawk, most falconers would agree that the musket (male sparrowhawk) will test even the most experienced of austringers. Modern, experienced austringers will prefer an imprinted hawk (see page 136), as this makes these birds slightly easier to handle and train. However, no amount of imprinting will ever make this bird easy.

THE GOSHAWK (*Accipiter gentilis*)

Often described as 'death on wings' or a 'feathered Exocet missile', the goshawk is an extremely fast and lethal bird. As mentioned earlier, however, this is not a bird for a novice, who will almost certainly spoil the bird, which will never realise its full potential. It is also one of the birds to which almost every novice aspires (as is the peregrine falcon) while not understanding just what is necessary to successfully train and fly a goshawk as a falconry bird.

In order to fly a goshawk properly, it is essential that the hawk be as sharp as possible, and it is also essential that such a bird is then carried on the fist for some time before being slipped, if one is to have a chance of avoiding the loss of the hawk. If the hawk is flown too high, then it will refuse difficult quarry, although it may well pursue, and often catch, easier stuff. However, this is not a well-trained goshawk, but sadly many austringers will never better this.

A bird of woodland, a well-trained goshawk is capable of taking a wide range of quarry, including rabbit, hare, duck, pheasant, partridge, pigeon, rook and crow and there have even been reports of successful flights at red grouse and geese. Without a doubt, it is the skill of the austringer which will bring out the best in a goshawk; siblings trained by different austringers may well show completely different traits, and one hawk's strength may be another hawk's weakness.

I cannot emphasise enough that goshawks, along with sparrowhawks, are not suitable for everyone, and certainly not for any beginner or novice austringer.

THE BLACK SPARROWHAWK (*Accipiter melnoleucus*)

This species is quite popular with experienced austringers within the UK, and occupies a position somewhere about halfway between a sparrowhawk and a goshawk. These birds are hyperactive and do not take kindly to being kept tethered, developing severe leg and foot problems unless equipped with very broad aylmeris and a bumper leash. Even when free-lofted, life is not easy with this species, since a black sparrowhawk kept in an aviary with a netted roof will quickly destroy its feathers, making it incapable of good flights.

Probably due to their size, this species is not suitable for use on ground game, although a female may occasionally take rabbit. Against feathered quarry, these hawks are good and very fast, being capable of taking on quite long slips, which makes them very exciting birds to fly.

A goshawk (*Accipiter gentilis*).

In the author's opinion, these hawks are even more difficult to train and fly for falconry purposes than the sparrowhawk, and only austringers with a great deal of experience of a large number of accipiters should attempt to train these birds.

BROADWINGS

HARRIS' OR BAY-WINGED HAWK (*Parabuteo unicinctus*)

Named by John James Audubon after his supporter, Dr Edward Harris, who sponsored and accompanied Audubon's 1843 Missouri River Expedition, when the species was discovered. All too often, this hawk is referred to erroneously as a Harris hawk, i.e. without the apostrophe.

Without a doubt, this species is one of the best hawks currently flown in the UK, although some experienced/older austringers will decry them as being 'beginners' birds'. The author considers the Harris' hawk to be the most versatile bird flown by falconers in the UK. The species is quite capable of flying direct pursuits or soaring, and taking quarry as diverse as hares, ducks and game birds in the hands of an experienced austringer. At the same time, the Harris' hawk is undoubtedly the best species for a beginner to take on, although such a handler/trainer will never bring out the best in the hawk.

Harris' hawks come from central and southern America, i.e. Argentina, Bolivia, Brazil, Chile, Colombia, Costa Rica, Ecuador, El Salvador, Guatemala, Honduras, Mexico, Nicaragua, Panama, Paraguay, Peru, Suriname, Uruguay and Venezuela and the southern parts of the United States of America. The species occupies a wide range of habitat, i.e. forest, scrubland, grassland and desert.

The largest specimens come from the north of the range, and are often referred to as 'superiors'. For various reasons, many falconers desire the largest specimens, even though the smaller ones are still more than capable of performing well.

Harris' hawks are unique in the proper sense of that word – there are no other birds like them (at least as far as we have so far discovered). In the wild, these hawks live in groups, consisting of the parent pair, last year's young and this year's young. They act, work and hunt collectively, i.e. in a true team. These hawks have been reported as sitting on the large cacti of the deserts and 'stacking'. This strange and unique behaviour involves the hawks sitting on each other's backs, often up to three high. It is believed that this action is taken either due to lack of roosting space, or as a method of still hunting (where the hawks sit and ambush their prey). The latter would give the hawks slightly more height and so allow them to see further, and also gain speed more quickly as they launch themselves after their quarry.

When hunting in the wild, Harris' hawks will use teamwork to quite literally ambush their quarry, with the smaller males often taking to the floor, running along and chasing the quarry towards other members of the pack, that may be sitting on the ground or on cacti, etc.

Because they are gregarious birds, Harris' hawks communicate, and can be quite vocal, even when in captivity. Normally, when hawks are vocal towards the falconer, it is believed that the bird has been wrongly imprinted, and these birds are often referred to as screamers. However, in the case of the vast majority of Harris' hawks, this is not the reason – the hawks simply see the falconer as a member of their pack and communicate accordingly. Another form of communication among a pack of Harris' hawks is tail shaking. In adult/mature Harris' hawks, the tail, or train, has a black stripe with a white stripe both above and below. As with most predators, the eyes of the Harris' hawk are attracted to movement, and the wagging of the tail is an excellent, silent method of letting the pack know where each individual is at any time.

When used as falconry birds, these hawks carry out similar behaviour and will happily stack on a tree, a fence or even the austringer's arm. When hunting, the Harris' hawk's teamwork really shows, and can give great sport. When hunted as a group or pack, or even as a cast (i.e. two hawks), these birds show what teamwork is about. While a female Harris' hawk will happily take a hare, a male will not. However, when two or more Harris's hawks are flown and hunted together, even a male will take on a hare, in the sure knowledge that he will be joined and assisted by the other hawk(s) in the pack. Where males and females are hunted together, a slightly different type of behaviour is seen, and this can best be illustrated by the story of a hunting day we held here at The National Falconry School.

We had four guests on the day, and so took out four hawks – two males and two females – with each guest carrying a hawk until we got into the wood we were working. At this stage, all four birds were lofted, i.e. cast into the branches of the trees in the wood. Usually on such hunting days, we take one or more of our dogs: we use English springer spaniels, a superb breed for this kind of hunting. These spaniels quarter the area, using their amazing sense of smell to find game hidden in the undergrowth, at which time they 'spring' or flush the game, and then drop into the sitting or lying position, in order to allow the hawk to run or fly down the quarry. On this particular day, however, the owner of the land had asked us not to take any dogs, as he was in the middle of a delicate piece of negotiation with his tenant farmer, who disliked having dogs on 'his' farm.

The wood was teeming with pheasants, but with no dog to flush them, they were sitting tight in areas where we humans could not get to encourage them to take to their wings. After about twenty metres of frustrating walking through the wood, with pheasants being tantalising close, but stalwartly refusing to flush, the Harris' hawks decided that they could do better than us humans. The males, smaller and more agile than their sisters, dropped to the floor, and began running under the bushes and other cover; immediately this started, the pheasants decided that they should take to the wing in an effort to outdistance their hunters. As the pheasants began to take off, the females, sitting waiting in the branches above the pheasants, dropped down on the game birds with deadly force. This action continued through the wood and, while many pheasants lived to see another day, we had several excellent slips, resulting in several pheasants destined for the casserole dish later that week.

I have also witnessed my own Harris' hawks carry out ambushes on rabbits, flushed from their warren by ferrets, resulting in more than one large rabbit pie.

One of the 'faults' which is attributed to the Harris' hawk by falconers who do not like this bird, is that, according to these people, Harris' hawks do not like dogs. This statement is backed up with the assertion that, in the wild, the Harris' hawk's only real competitor is the coyote, and it therefore follows, goes the argument, that in captivity, Harris' hawks will never take to working with dogs. Rubbish! If dog and hawk are properly introduced, then there is no reason why the relationship should not be good. (See Chapter 6 for more on this subject.)

The Harris' hawk is much underrated. I am certain that if more falconers were to put aside their preconceived ideas and prejudices about this bird, it would soon become universally accepted as *the* hawk.

THE EURASIAN OR COMMON BUZZARD (*Buteo buteo*)

Another species which was once recommended as a suitable hawk for a beginner to learn on, this buzzard has fallen out of favour with all but its most ardent fans. Some authorities still recommend this species, warning that starting with a Harris's hawk will lull the novice into a false sense of security, as Harris's hawks are 'too easy'.

I cannot agree with this sentiment. Rather than using the term 'easy', I prefer to use the terms 'biddable' and 'trainable'. How these attributes can be seen as anything other than positive baffles me completely.

Common buzzards tend not to want to work too hard, unless an inordinate amount of effort, work and time has been put in by the austringer. Even when a buzzard has been conditioned to such a degree that it could be described as 'being in yarak' (see Appendix 2), it will only take young rabbits, rats and similar small quarry. And yet it will take far more effort, time and skill to bring a common buzzard to this condition than it will to bring a Harris' hawk to yarak and, as stated earlier, the Harris' hawk is capable of much more sport.

In my experience, when a beginner starts his falconry career with a common buzzard, the bird is soon outgrown, and ends up on the scrap heap. The austringer has invested quite a bit of money (today, common buzzards can fetch almost as much as some Harris' hawks), lots of time and mountains of effort, and has very little to show for this investment when the bird is taken into the field. At this stage, the austringer decides to get rid of the unwanted buzzard, but will soon find that no one will want to buy such a bird. And so, the austringer is left with a bird that does not cut the mustard, still needs housing and feeding, and may well live in excess of twenty years. Much better to start with a Harris' hawk – and it may well be the only species you will need.

A common or Eurasian buzzard (*Buteo buteo*).

THE RED-TAILED BUZZARD (*Buteo jamaicensis*)

Another hawk often recommended as suitable for a beginner. I have heard one authority state that this species is by far the best as, because of the hawk's truculent nature, an austringer learning his trade with such a bird will have many problems, and thus be a better falconer for those bad experiences. Again, I cannot go along with this idea, as I am a big believer that success breeds success, while failure breeds failure. I am also acutely aware that when a novice falconer makes mistakes, they could result in an unwanted or dumped hawk, or even a dead hawk. Keep to the KISS principle – Keep It Short and Simple – and you will not go far wrong, and the chances of killing a hawk through your lack of knowledge, skill or through sheer incompetence will be minimised.

Red-tailed buzzards (referred to as red-tailed hawks by Americans) seem, to me, to have many of the disadvantages of the goshawk – they tend to be moody and bad-tempered – without the advantages of the Harris' hawk. I believe these hawks make good second birds, but for them to do well, the austringer must have a reasonable amount of skill and experience. When a novice takes up such a bird for training as his first hawk, mistakes are inevitable. An eyas tends to become very sticky footed, and the sheer strength of a red-tailed buzzard can often be enough to put off all but the most resilient of newcomers to the sport. The hawk's strength is usually made clear to the novice when the bird foots the ungloved hand or arm of the would-be falconer.

Adherents of this hawk will point out that, in the United States of America, this species is the most commonly selected bird for a beginner. What these people almost always fail to mention is that, in the US, novice falconers are required (by law) to serve a two-year apprenticeship with a master falconer, thereby giving the novice falconer a vast amount of experience on tap. In addition, the red-tailed buzzards flown by the Americans differ from those flown in the UK, as UK birds are captive bred, whereas in the US, the falconer is allowed to take passage birds from the wild, and is forbidden from starting his falconry career with an eyas. The differences in these two types of the same species are immense.

THE FERRUGINOUS BUZZARD (*Buteo regalis*)

Referred to as the ferruginous hawk in America, many people with experience of this hawk are confident that it should be reclassified as an eagle, as many of its characteristics are reminiscent of eagles. Indeed, many North American falconers, such as Frank Beebe, refer to this bird as the ferruginous eagle. Hopefully, DNA analysis will help prove the bird's true status in the not-too-distant future.

Not a beginner's bird, the ferruginous can be extremely bad tempered and suffers from small feet. The male's feet are so small that he is next to useless in the hunting field, although the female can, and often does, show herself to be capable of taking full-grown rabbits. These hawks can be extremely fast, using their immensely powerful legs to help get airborne from the ground, fist or branch, and they perform well when used in country resembling their native land – open country. Many ferruginous buzzards refuse to go into trees, and so their use in woodland should not be considered.

Slow to start, the ferruginous buzzard soon learns and then is easy to enter, although they prefer to take furred rather than feathered quarry.

Ferruginous buzzards can be extremely difficult to man (see Manning, page 60) and, almost without exception, they do not enjoy sitting on the fist, constantly baiting and impersonating bats at roost as they hang upside down from the austringer's gloved hand. Neither do these hawks like sitting on blocks or bows, preferring to sit on the ground next to the perch.

THE GOLDEN EAGLE (*Aquila chrysaetos*)

With any hawk used for falconry purposes, it is important to ensure that one has the correct country over which to hunt the bird. With golden eagles, this means large areas of open, hilly countryside – areas to which very few austringers will ever have access. Consequently, this hawk is not suitable for most falconers, even though many will openly state that they aspire towards ownership and use of this magnificent bird.

At the risk of upsetting some readers, I feel that many falconers who choose to attempt to train and fly a golden eagle, somehow feel that possessing such a bird will make them appear even bigger in the eyes of onlookers, in the same way that some people – usually men – have to have a large, fierce breed of dog. For many, it is these very aspects of the golden eagle – size and strength – that render them as unsuitable birds for those particular falconers. Golden eagles will require extremely large weathering/aviaries, a strong falconer to carry them and a big, thick, strong glove to protect the falconer's hand (and arm) from the eagle's immensely powerful talons.

All eagles are extremely moody, and can become very territorial, leading to physical brawls between eagle and falconer. While some falconers will warn never to have an imprinted eagle, others will not have anything but an imprinted eagle, each citing the eagle's moods as a reason for their choice. I have only trained and flown four eagles, only one of which was imprinted, and feel unqualified to comment on this aspect of eagles. However, there are many good books which detail imprinting methods, including their use in the training of eagles (see Bibliography, page 165).

All-in-all, golden eagles are best left to those fortunate few who have the time, experience, skill and vast amounts of open, hilly countryside over which to fly this magnificent bird. Flying eagles is a very specialised area of falconry, and there are several good books on the subject (see Bibliography, page 165).

THE TAWNY EAGLE (*Aquila rapax*) and THE STEPPES EAGLE (*Aquila nipalensis*)

These two eagles, believed by many to be subspecies of the same bird, are much smaller and easier to train and fly than their large cousin, the golden eagle. Even so, as with all eagles, these birds can be extremely moody and often have tantrums, making them difficult birds for all but experienced austringers.

There are two distinct 'races' of the tawny eagle – the Indian and the African, with the former being somewhat smaller and slighter than the African. In addition, there are several colour phases in both races. The steppes eagle is slightly bigger than the tawny, but seems to lack the 'zip' that one often finds with tawny eagles.

When used as falconry birds, when properly trained and brought to yarak, both of these species are well able to take a wide variety of game, and excel at slope soaring after rabbit and hare.

A female African tawny eagle: eagles are large and strong and require an experienced falconer.

LONGWINGS

THE MERLIN (*Falco columbarius*)

Merlins are tiny, and need an extremely experienced and skilled falconer to train them successfully. With an unusually high metabolic rate, these birds need to be weighed, flown, exercised and fed twice daily. Even then, the diet must consist of high protein foods, such as mice and rats, etc. and the weighing of the hawk must be extremely accurate.

For the purposes of this book, I do not deem the merlin as being useful for practical hawking, and will not go into further details about this diminutive but definitely charismatic hawk. Those with a genuine interest in this species will find more information in books listed in the Bibliography (see page 165).

THE LANNER FALCON (*Falco biarmicus*)

The lanner falcon is often recommended as the first longwing for an aspiring falconer, as they are fairly straightforward to train. Although these small longwings will wait on well, their small size makes them less useful than, say, a peregrine, although quite capable of taking partridge.

At one time, the lanner was an extremely popular bird with UK falconers, although never excelling at game hawking. However, the species then fell out of favour and the numbers being bred diminished greatly. I feel that this was mainly due to their use in producing hybrids, with the peregrine x lanner hybrid being an extremely useful hawk. Recently, more lanners have been bred and their prices have risen to reflect their relative scarcity.

THE LUGGER OR LAGGAR FALCON (*Falco jugger*)

The lugger, very much a Jekyll and Hyde character, being extremely moody and rather unpredictable, is a superb species to fly to the lure, for demonstrations, displays and similar uses. The lugger has never really caught on as a true falconry bird within the UK falconry fraternity. However, as with the peregrine, hybrids have proven quite popular.

Unfortunately, the number of luggers within the UK is extremely small and most are related. This has obviously resulted in a very tiny gene pool and consequent poor breeding of this species.

THE PEREGRINE FALCON (*Falco peregrinus*)

The peregrine (and its many subspecies), is among the most popular and useful falconry bird in the UK, if not the world as a whole. They are flown at a vast range of quarry – crow, duck, grouse, gulls, magpie, partridge, pheasant, pigeon, ptarmigan, rook, snipe, woodcock – but rarely take mammals, as befits a hawk which specialises in a steep, vertical stoop at over 250 kph (150 mph).

Obviously, and unsurprisingly, the peregrine is considered as the best longwing to fly against quarry within the UK, the bird's hard feathers serving well in the British climate. A slow-maturing hawk, the peregrine is popular both in its pure form and as a bird used in producing top quality hybrids.

THE PRAIRIE FALCON (*Falco mexicanus*)

This American longwing has never really had a good following in the UK, although it is occasionally used for producing hybrids. In my experience, these birds tend to be aggressive and unpredictable in their moods and behaviour. A lot of skill and patience is required to train and enter a prairie falcon.

THE SAKER FALCON (*Falco cherrug*)

A very large hawk, the saker is not overly popular among British falconers, although the species is often used for producing hybrids (with peregrines, gyr, etc.). There is a legend among UK falconers that, if one were to fly a saker during spring (April and May) or autumn (August and September) – the times of year that the wild saker would be migrating, then the hawk would invariably be lost. I have flown several sakers over the years, and have never encountered this phenomenon, but others assure me that they have and I have simply been very lucky.

With a good temperament, the saker can often mislead the inexperienced falconer, and lull him or her into a false sense of security, and it is therefore essential to fly this species very fine, i.e. very close to its flying weight, if one is not to spend many hours searching for the lost hawk with the yagi.

In the Middle East, the saker is considered to be a superb hawk for falconry, although few British falconers would concur with this opinion.

THE GYR FALCON (*Falco rusticolus*)

The gyr falcon is the largest species of falcon, and the fastest in a straight line. In the wild, the gyr occupies a subarctic circumpolar territory. Coming in various colour phases, the gyr is a magnificent-looking bird which has many adherents. These huge hawks can be flown out of the hood (e.g. at rook, crows or even gulls), and can also be trained to wait on for use against game birds. However, when employed for the latter task, gyr falcons have a rather nasty habit of raking downwind, rather than wait on in the way that a peregrine falcon will. This raking away allows the game bird to see its opportunity to escape, which it will promptly attempt to do. When the gyr sees this, it will turn on its incredible speed, and attempt to fly down the game bird in a chase. As, for most falconers, the sheer thrill of game hawking is to see the dramatic vertical stoop of the falcon, such a chase is something of an anticlimax.

In days past, the only way to get one or more gyr falcons was to send an expedition to the Arctic to catch and bring back the birds – a colossally expensive undertaking. Today, more and more falconers are breeding these birds in captivity, and the gyr falcon remains a highly desirable acquisition to many falconers, even though they are not the best birds for falconry purposes, as can be seen in records from falconers over the years.

In addition, the captive gyr falcon suffers a wide range of health problems and cannot tolerate environmental conditions which feature heat, humidity or dust. Gyrs kept in such conditions are highly susceptible to respiratory diseases such as aspergillosis. (See Chapter 9 First Aid and Health). Gyr falcons also need good perches if they are not to suffer from bumble foot and similar problems.

The gyr falcon is a wilful and extremely inquisitive hawk, and will bear grudges against any falconer who upsets it. It is also true that, as gyrs require open country for their flights, very few falconers will ever be able to do justice to this bird.

SEXUAL DIMORPHISM

All birds of prey will differ in size and shape between the sexes. Whereas in mammals, it is the male which is usually larger than the female, in raptors the opposite is true, with females being up to a third larger than males of the same species. This phenomenon is referred to as 'reversed sexual dimorphism'. It is from this size difference that the name for a male bird – a tiercel – is derived. Traditionally, this term was given only to the male peregrine, while the female was known simply as the falcon. Modern usage is to refer to all female members of the genus *Falco* as falcons, and all the males as tiercels. Some falconers will use the term tiercel, which derives from a French word meaning 'one third', for any male bird of prey, whether they be falcons, hawks or eagles, etc.

As the training of raptors requires careful management of the bird's weight, males will be more difficult to train than females of the same species, as the margin of error between the bird being too heavy or too light will be that much smaller.

HYBRIDS

Some years ago, falconers discovered the art of artificial insemination (AI), and since then, this procedure has been used to produce a wide range of hybrid hawks. AI has been used successfully to hybridise falcons, hawks, buzzards and eagles and, unlike many mammal species, all of the offspring are fertile, illustrating the fact that all species in each genus of birds of prey are interfertile.

Responsible hawk breeders will only cross species to produce better birds for specific tasks, although I have seen some evidence of those who seem to cross species

A hybrid, long-winged hawk (peregrine x lugger) flying. Note the hawk's bell (on right leg) and flying jesses.

simply because they are able to, without any consideration as to what use the offspring of such crosses may be put.

THE KESTREL (*Falco tunniculus*)

Readers will no doubt notice that the Eurasian Kestrel (*Falco tunniculus*) is missing from the above lists – this is intentional, and not an oversight on the author's part. This book relates to practical hawking and, with the best will in the world, no falconer can claim to have used this species for hawking.

Many older falconers began their falconry career with one of these diminutive birds, as I did, way back in the 1960s. That most of these kestrels, taken from the wild as was then the legal custom, did not live very long in captivity is a sad fact, and an indication of how difficult this species is for a beginner or novice to manage correctly. It is also an indication that, in those days of yesteryear, there were not suitable species with which the tyro (beginner) falconer could learn his trade without often inflicting unintentional cruelty on the birds.

Birds of prey are trained through the management of the bird's weight: the smaller the species, the less the margin for error. On average, a kestrel will fly at about 150 grammes (about 5 ounces) rendering the margin to a very small amount between a bird which is 'high' or in high condition (i.e. too heavy) and thus will not fly to the falconer, and a bird which is 'low' or in low condition (i.e. too light) and so cannot fly to the falconer as it is too weak. A novice falconer would be hard pushed to manage the bird's weight in order to keep the hawk at its correct flying weight, unless serving a proper apprenticeship and having a master falconer to guide him.

OWLS

Again, some readers may wonder why I have not mentioned owls. The answer is simple – these are most definitely *not* falconry birds.

While many falconers will keep and often train owls, these birds will be flown simply for pleasure and not hunted. While some people may claim that the eagle owls, most notably the Eurasian eagle owl (*Bubo bubo*), the largest species of owl in the world, can be used for hunting and catching foxes, this is not true. In more than forty years of hawking, I have never witnessed such a bird take quarry of this type. Neither can I find references to any wild eagle owl taking foxes, other than very small cubs.

There are, of course, many other species of hawk flown by falconers, but I feel that the foregoing has given a taste of the most common/popular species used by British falconers. As will be seen, there are few species with a universal use and most have differing temperaments, training requirements and hunting preferences.

In the following pages, most of the information relates to all falconry birds, although I have specifically and intentionally chosen to feature the UK's most popular and successful falconry bird – the Harris' hawk. Where information and details for this species differ enormously from that for other species, I have tried to indicate this and given relevant information.

A young tawny owlet (*Strix aluco*); with lots of 'Aaaaah' appeal, it is easy to see why people are tempted to keep these birds as pets, but they are not suitable for falconry.

CHAPTER 3
GENERAL HUSBANDRY

GENERAL PRINCIPLES

All animals kept in captivity should be given the opportunity to have a good quality of life and, in the UK, these principles are encapsulated within a code known as 'The Five Provisions'.

The Five Provisions

1. Provision of food and water.
2. Provision of a suitable environment.
3. Provision of animal healthcare.
4. Provision of protection from fear and distress.
5. Provision of an opportunity to express most normal behaviours.

The reader will see that these provisions really are common sense, and none should cause any problems to falconers.

FEEDING

As falconry birds are trained and controlled by careful management of their weight, it will be appreciated that diet is a very important part of this management. To those people who do not understand/accept/agree with what we, as falconers, do then it might seem that we do not feed our hawks correctly nor adequately. Indeed, I have heard opponents of falconry state that falconers 'starve their birds into submission' – rubbish. If a hawk is starving it will not have the strength to fly, so falconers cannot achieve their aim by this method. When asked about this by non-falconers, I like to explain that we simply keep an edge on our hawks' appetites, carefully monitoring and controlling the type and amount of food fed to the birds, and thus keeping the birds at their optimum fitness – which is a condition obviously millions of miles away from starvation.

FREQUENCY

With most species of hawk, it is common practice to feed the bird once daily, once the hawk is fully grown. If a young, immature hawk is fed too little, its feathers will not grow correctly, leaving marks on the feathers, or making them deformed in some other way. Because a lack of food leads to distress with any animal, the bird is said to fret, and the marks are known as fret marks or lines.

The exceptions are hawks such as the merlin, which have a very high metabolic rate, and so need feeding/exercising twice daily, as mentioned in Chapter 2.

It is normal, once the hawk is trained, to give this feed as part of the hawk's daily training/flying/working period.

A BALANCED DIET

Before going any further, it is worth considering what constitutes a 'balanced diet' for a hawk. All animals require certain items in their diet, with quite large differences between species. All animals require water, fat, carbohydrate, protein, fibre, some minerals and some vitamins. These requirements are not static: they will change with the animal's age, lifestyle and physiological state, and so they will need to be adjusted and 'tweaked' throughout the animal's life. An animal fed on a balanced diet will lead a long, active and healthy life, more than repaying you for the cost of its diet. Whilst feeding an imbalanced diet may not seem to cause problems for some animals, the deleterious effects will be readily observed in a breeding programme or during a hawk's moult. At both of these times, the animal will require different dietary constituents than it would at normal times.

The main components of a balanced diet are:

- Proteins
- Vitamins
- Minerals
- Carbohydrates
- Fats
- Fibre
- Water

Proteins

Proteins are made from amino acids, are essential for growth and tissue maintenance, and are available to the hawk via meat/flesh. There are many different proteins, all consisting of different arrangements of about some twenty-three amino acids, but it is not necessary to differentiate between them here, except to emphasise that the hawks are obligate carnivores, i.e. they are designed to eat, and properly digest, meat/flesh.

It should be obvious that, while all hawks require a high-protein diet, this is even more important when considering breeding birds, their young and young hawks in general. Also, hawks in moult will require higher levels of protein to assist in a proper moult, i.e. the shedding and re-growth of feathers.

Carbohydrates

Carbohydrates provide the hawk's body with heat and material for growth. Carbohydrates are made up of carbon, hydrogen and oxygen (which combine to form cellulose, starch and sugar) and excess amounts are stored as fat in the body, which can therefore lead to obesity if fed in excess on a regular basis. Obesity can and does cause medical problems, and will also inevitably lead to difficulties in a hawk's breeding. Carbohydrates are present in plant material: such material is available to hawks and carnivores via the stomach contents of their prey, as well as by direct ingestion of other plant material.

Vitamins

Vitamins, chemical compounds essential for growth, health, normal metabolism and general physical well-being, obviously play an important part in the well-being of a hawk. Many vitamins play an important part in completing essential chemical reactions in the body, forming parts of enzymes (chemical catalysts). Some vitamins form parts of hormones, which are the chemical substances that promote the health of the body and reproduction.

Vitamins are divided into two types – water-soluble and fat-soluble.

1. Water-soluble vitamins (B and C) cannot be stored in the body. Excess water-soluble vitamins are excreted, so every day's food intake must contain the day's requirements of these vitamins for the hawk.
2. Fat-soluble vitamins (A, D, E and K) can be stored in the body. If more are taken in at one time than the hawk needs, fat-soluble vitamins can be stored for use when the body needs them. It should be noted, however, that an excess of such vitamins may cause toxic levels to accumulate in storage areas such as the liver, and thus may lead to long-term physical problems.

A lack of, or an insufficiency of, any vitamin is known as avitaminosis, and an excess of a vitamin is referred to as hypervitaminosis. A lack of essential vitamins will be detrimental to a hawk's health.

Avitaminosis A (insufficient amounts of vitamin A) in a hawk will result in poor growth, muscular incoordination and poor night vision. Avitaminosis A is also linked to opaqueness of the hawk's eye lenses. An excellent source of vitamin A for hawks is liver.

Vitamin B is a complex of water-soluble vitamins, including biotin, choline, folacin, niacin, thiamin, riboflavin, pantothenic acid, pyridoxine and vitamin B_{12}. Avitaminosis B will manifest itself as anorexia, vomiting, poor movement, heart problems, poor weight gain, greying/lightening of feathers, conjunctivitis, poor circulation and many other symptoms.

Vitamin C is a potent antioxidant and is needed for growth, healthy body tissue, wound repair and an efficient immune system. Vitamin C also plays a part in the reduction of cholesterol levels and helps regulate blood pressure and the body's absorption of iron.

Vitamin D is often referred to as 'the sunshine vitamin', as some species can synthesise this vitamin if the animal is exposed to full daylight on a regular basis. The amount of vitamin D required is also dependent on the calcium:phosphorous ratio fed to the hawks. Abnormal bone development is a typical effect of avitaminosis D.

Vitamin E is found in the yolk of eggs (or in our case, in the yolk sac of day-old chicks) and in certain vegetable oils. A lack of this vitamin can cause infertility, heart and circulation problems, and skin complaints; feeding too many eggs (yolk sacs) can also cause problems.

Vitamin K is necessary for normal blood clotting.

Fat

Fat affects the palatability of food and provides the hawk's body with energy but, given too much, the body will store fat in the tissues, which can lead to many problems, including breeding difficulties, heart problems and the retention of eggs. Fat gives approximately 2.4 times more energy (calories) per gram than does carbohydrate.

Minerals

The mineral calcium, essential for sound strong bones and the shells of eggs when breeding the hawks, is found in liver, milk and milk products, egg shells, fish and snails; calcium is also found in the bones and teeth of all animals. Phosphorous is found in liver, milk and milk products, and fish, and is also essential for bones. When feeding a hawk, ensuring that the feed contains large quantities of bone will give the hawk sufficient calcium. This is extremely important during breeding (calcium forming the egg shell) and the moult. A lack of calcium will result in fret lines and/or deformed feathers.

Iron and copper are both essential to hawks (copper is necessary for the hawk's body to absorb iron, an essential element of haemoglobin – the oxygen-carrying constituent of a hawk's red blood cells). A lack of these minerals can result in emaciation, anaemia, poor feather quality and colouration.

Magnesium deficiency in hawks may result in anorexia, poor weight gain, irritability or weak muscles.

Insufficient levels of potassium in a hawk's diet may result in poor/retarded growth, muscular paralysis or restlessness.

Sodium and chlorine are essential to a hawk's normal physiological performance. Deficiencies may result in a number of symptoms, including tiredness, retarded growth, weight loss, excessive water intake and dry, flaky skin.

Zinc helps prevent poor growth, anorexia and emaciation.

As can be seen from the foregoing information, a balanced and truly complete diet for hawks is complicated, and most falconers will struggle to provide this essential dietary regime unless they are providing a mixture of feeds, complemented with extra vitamins and minerals.

OLFACTORY IMPRINTING

It is worth noting that hawks will develop feeding tastes and preferences at an early age: in other words, they will develop a liking for the foods eaten while young, and these tastes will stay with them throughout their life, a process known as 'olfactory imprinting'. This is a process in which the exposure of animals to olfactory cues during specific and restricted time windows leaves a permanent memory (known as an 'olfactory imprint') which shapes the animal's behaviour upon encountering the olfactory cues at later times. This is the phenomenon that leads hawks fed solely on a diet of day-old chicks to refuse rats, mice, quail and other meats. It is obvious therefore, that all young hawks must be fed a variety of feeds from day one.

TYPES OF FEED

There is a range of foods that will suffice to give to hawks in general, but some are more suitable than others in different circumstances:

- Beef
- DOC – Day-old chick (cockerel)
- Game e.g. pheasant, quail
- Hare
- Moorhen
- Rabbit
- Rodent e.g. rat, mouse, etc.

Each type of meat will have a different calorific value, as follows:

FOOD TYPE	CALORIFIC VALUE
Beef	Medium
DOC	Medium
Game-bird	High
Hare	High
Moorhen	Very High
Quail	High
Rabbit	Low
Rats and Mice	Medium-High

As the different types of food have different calorific values, they will affect a hawk's weight differently. Obviously, then, in order to keep a hawk at flying weight will require less food of a high calorific value than it would food of a low calorific value.

As mentioned earlier, to keep hawks in the best of health and fitness, their diet must contain a variety of food. If feeding 'wild food' or game e.g. rabbit, hare, pheasant, moorhen, etc., this should be checked to ensure that it does not contain lead shot. Even if you have caught the quarry using a hawk or a ferret, or shot it yourself using a rifle, it may still contain lead shot from previous encounters with hunters. It is vital that you always check before feeding any such game to your hawk, as any lead ingested by a hawk could kill it.

Freezing

Although fresh feed is far better – for both nutrition and palatability – all hawk feed can be frozen for storage, although this must be done while the meat is as fresh as possible. The ideal way to freeze meat for hawk feed is by blast freezing, but very few falconers have access to the machinery necessary for this procedure. Where freezing is being carried out in a domestic freezer, the carcass should be allowed to cool, and then placed in the freezer with the freezer set on 'boost'. The boost should be left running until the carcasses have all frozen solid. Failure to freeze meat properly can lead to a whole host of 'food poisoning' problems, as can re-freezing feed which has defrosted.

Thawing

When thawing food from the freezer, it is important to ensure that it is not allowed to come into contact with flies as this, too, could cause health problems for the hawks. We use a large, airtight plastic box which is placed well away from sunlight. We put the frozen feed into the box on the day before it is needed, and then store the box in an area where the ambient temperature will enable the food to defrost properly within 24 hours. Any defrosted feed should be used as soon as possible after defrosting.

Cast or Casting

In the same way that mammals require fibre (roughage) to help keep their digestive systems working correctly, hawks should be fed fibre in the form of meat covered with feather or fur, properly known as cast or casting. This casting should be fed at least twice weekly, although most falconers will feed their hawks with casting every day. The casting is not digested by the hawk but will be regurgitated about 24 hours after being fed. When flying/exercising the hawk, it is important that this pellet is cast before such exercise.

Supplementation

No matter how wide a variety of feed is given to a hawk, it is still highly probable that the bird's diet is lacking in some essential minerals and/or vitamins. Such deficiencies will be most noticeable during the moult and when the bird is used for breeding, and it is at such times that supplementation is necessary.

While it is possible to buy general 'multi-vitamin and mineral' supplements, there is now a wide range of supplements specifically designed and formulated for birds at various life stages, and these are to be recommended. True, such specialised items will cost a little more than general supplements, but the extra cost is more than justified for such specialisation. We feed such supplements twice weekly for our flying birds, but every other day for breeding birds and during the moult.

WATER

The importance of giving all hawks constant access to a supply of fresh, clean water cannot be over-emphasised: without such access, hawks will not thrive. When hawks have only limited access to potable (drinkable) water, the birds are in danger of kidney failure. Water is essential to help the kidneys function – getting rid of the toxic ammonia in the body and flushing it out of the body as urea contained within the mutes, which is composed mainly of water.

In medieval times, it was believed that hawks did not need to drink. The argument was based on the erroneous idea that, as hawks eat animal bodies containing large amounts of fluid, the hawks would get all of their water requirements from this source. A hawk which drank large amounts of water was referred to as a bowser, and this term has become 'boozer' in modern English.

Although the hawk feed will contain large amounts of water, it is not true that hawks should not be given water to drink, as all living things require water throughout their life. While some hawks seem never to drink, other hawks will drink small amounts when bathing. For this reason, a bath of clean, fresh water should be

Harris' hawks on the weathering ground of The National Falconry School in 1992. Note all hawks are on bow perches, and each has its own bath of clean water, for both bathing and/or drinking.

offered to every hawk whenever the weather permits. Even if a hawk refuses to use the bath, either for bathing or for drinking, it should still be given the opportunity on a regular, daily basis.

WEIGHT CONTROL

Weight control is the key to successful flights with a hawk; if the bird is correctly manned and at the correct weight, training should go along as planned.

There are three weights for a bird:

• Top Weight – the weight of the hawk when it is taken from the breeding aviary, at which time it will have been fed and eaten as much food as it wanted.
• Flying Weight – the weight at which the hawk has enough energy to be able to fly, yet still has an edge to its appetite which will make it want to fly.
• Dead Weight – a weight at which a hawk has insufficient energy to allow its body to function properly.

The rate at which a hawk's weight will drop depends on:

- Time between feeds
- Amount of food given
- Type of food given
- Amount of exercise
- Species
- Ambient temperature

A creance attached to the hawk's swivel. It is better to attach the creance directly to the jesses, as the weight of the swivel can cause the line to tangle when the hawk flies.

A hawk used for falconry purposes needs to be weighed every day prior to being fed (preferably at a strict 24-hour interval, i.e. the same time each day) and a record kept of its weight on that day. While some falconers use a notebook, especially if they have only a single hawk, with over fifty hawks we prefer to use a whiteboard for this. This allows us, at a glance, to see the pattern of any hawk's weight over a seven-day period.

Over a few days of this regime, a picture will start to appear detailing the hawk's progress compared to its weight. As a very general guide, a bird should not be reduced by any more than 15% of its top weight to reach its flying weight, since a greater weight loss is liable to cause health concerns for the hawk.

After a small weight loss, the hawk will step onto the falconer's fist. The next day, with more weight loss, the bird should jump the length of the leash. Eventually, the hawk will happily fly a hundred metres to the fist, while on the creance. At this time, the creance should be removed, and the hawk allowed free flight. As the hawk gets fitter, its weight will increase, as muscle weighs more than flab, and the hawk will require an increased feed ration.

It is important to continue weighing

the hawk on a regular, daily basis while it is used for falconry purposes, and to carefully monitor and record these weights. If it is seen that the hawk appears to have little 'staying power', losing its energy after a few flights, thought should be given to increasing its feed ration and raising its flying weight. Conversely, if the hawk appears hesitant at chasing quarry and/or returning to the falconer's fist, it may be necessary to decrease, by a small amount, the hawk's daily food ration and thereby decrease its flying weight. It takes a certain amount of experience to know when a hawk is misbehaving due to a lack of food or due to too much food.

HOUSING

There are various types of housing suitable for hawks, including:

- Aviaries
- Weatherings
- Mews

AVIARIES

Aviaries are large and designed to allow the hawk(s) freedom to fly. As such, they are useful for breeding hawks and also hawks in moult. While they can also be used to keep *trained* falconry hawks in good condition between work, they should not be used for young, untrained hawks. Such hawks, not properly trained and/or manned, are liable to panic and fly into the cage netting, causing themselves injury.

For breeding, many falconers prefer 'seclusion' or 'sky light' aviaries. These are aviaries where the walls of the structure are solid, with the only view for the hawks being of the sky, ensuring that passing humans and animals do not disturb the hawks during the crucial breeding times.

WEATHERINGS

Weatherings are smaller structures, designed to keep a tethered hawk in safety while allowing the hawk access to fresh air and the sights and sounds to which it will need to become accustomed ('manned').

MEWS

Traditionally a place where hawks were kept to moult, now a term used to describe a building where several hawks are kept, tethered, between flights.

GENERAL

Whichever type of enclosure one decides upon, it must be remembered that a hawk will spend much of its time in its 'cage', and so the housing should be given much thought. Do not be tempted to build 'temporary' housing structures as these tend, all too often, to become permanent. Whatever type of housing one considers for one's hawk, it should be weatherproof, be easy to clean and maintain, draughtproof, and wholly suitable for the species and individual.

The parameters which should be borne in mind when making the decision as to what type of housing one is to use for one's hawks include:

- Size
- Location/Positioning
- Materials and construction

Size

I do not feel it right to state 'minimum' or 'recommended' sizes, since these become, all too often, the 'standard'. Where a weathering is used, the structure should be large enough to allow the bird to open its wings in any direction, i.e. front to back or side to side. Indeed, in the UK, animal welfare regulations make it unlawful to keep a bird in a 'cage' in which the bird cannot spread its wings, except when the bird is kept in such a cage for transport, medical reasons or for exhibition.

On average, the weathering should be about two metres (approximately six feet) square, with a block/bow (perch) in the centre. This size will need to be increased for the larger species, such as eagles, but should be fine for most of the commonly flown hawks, buzzards and falcons.

In order to make life easier, the height should be suitable for a human to stand in, without having to bend, as this will help make cleaning and maintenance easier. I like my weatherings to have a sloping roof (sloping to the rear) to prevent the build-up of water on the roof.

Materials and construction

Undoubtedly the most common material for the average do-it-yourself enthusiast is wood. This material is easy to work with, relatively cheap and easily available. It is not waterproof, but can be made so by the application of paints and similar materials.

When building in wood, ensure that the timber used is of sufficient thickness and quality. Plywood is probably the most commonly used type of timber, and this should be the type designed for outdoor use, or 'marine quality plywood': 9 mm or 12 mm are good thicknesses for most applications. Any paint used must be non-toxic and 100% 'animal safe'. Even though hawks will not chew wood, they could still ingest paint, etc. dislodged by their everyday activities, and this is particularly so on feed ledges, etc.

When building walls of wood, it is best to first build a small wall of concrete blocks as a base. This should be at least two to three blocks high. A concrete floor will also help ensure that the aviary or weathering can be kept clean with relative ease. This concrete base should slope to one end of the construction and a drain can be built in at this point. This will allow the structure to be cleaned with a power hose or similar, and the water will run into the drain.

The wooden sides of the building should be securely bolted to the block wall, using metal angle and screws or nuts and bolts. Nails should not be used, as these have a habit of loosening with disastrous consequences. Special care should be used when fitting the roof, as this is likely to catch the wind, and may be blown off in gales. We tend to build a second roof, using galvanised wire netting, about 200 mm (8 inches) below the external roof. This acts as a safeguard should the external roof be blown off.

The external roof, if of solid construction, should be covered with top quality felt and tar (if made of wood). It is, however, far better to use corrugated (or similar) metal or plastic which will not require felting. If metal is used, it will need to be insulated on the inside in order to prevent extremes of temperature within the construction. It is possible to buy 'plastic' corrugated roofing which is specifically designed to act as a thermal barrier, and this does not require insulation.

Location/Positioning

While most hawks can cope adequately with fairly cold conditions, they are not necessarily happy in such a state of affairs. Hawks, however, cannot cope with high temperatures, draughts or damp, and all these factors should be considered when planning the location and positioning of the weathering, etc. Weatherings and suchlike should not be placed in an area where it – and the hawk – will be subjected to the full heat of the midday sun, and neither must it be in an area swept by cold winds. In addition, it must be made waterproof (see previous section) if the inhabitants are to be comfortable and healthy.

Take into account the prevailing winds in your locale, and ensure that the back of the weathering faces in that direction, or that some form of windbreak or shelter is provided to prevent wind chill. Although hawks cannot tolerate high temperatures, they do appreciate a little time to 'soak up the rays' and bask in the gentle warmth of early morning sunshine and, if possible, the weathering should be positioned to allow for this.

The position of the weathering must also take into account the human(s) who will need to visit it and its inmate(s) on a regular basis, and service the weathering and the hawk(s). A long walk through trees and across grass may seem pleasant in the summer months, but will take on a whole new perspective in the depths of winter. Where I live, we regularly get large falls of snow and sub-zero temperatures for over three months of every year, and long, unnecessary walks are not something to look forward to.

A path made of paving stones, concrete or even pebbles, will help prevent the human carers having to plough through acres of mud to get to the weathering.

TEMPERATURE REGULATION

Where hawks are kept in a building, i.e. a mews, some form of temperature control is essential, especially where a hawk is tethered throughout the day and/or night. We utilise oil-filled radiators, convection heaters and storage heaters in our mews to keep the ambient temperature at about 22 °C. Placing a heat bulb above each perch will also help ensure that the hawks are kept at comfortable temperatures during the cold winter months. This heat bulb should have a protective grid between it and the hawk, and the holder should be placed about 450 mm (18 inches) above the hawk's head. We use a heater holder which has the facility to be switched from full- to half-power – it is usually sufficient to use at half-power. If the heat is too intense, it can cause problems for the hawk. To ensure that the heaters are operating at all times when needed, we have had the electrical circuit for the heaters installed as separate from the standard circuits in the mews. This circuit is connected to a thermostat, which will automatically operate the heaters when the temperature (at the thermostat) falls to a pre-designated level. In some countries, such installations have to be made by suitably qualified electricians, but if the reader is attempting such work, he/she must be competent or the consequences could be dire.

In order to keep mews and weatherings comfortable in the heat of the summer, adequate ventilation is essential. In our mews, we have a circuit specifically for a series of extractor fans, and these are operated via a suitably placed thermostat, which can, if necessary, be manually overridden.

All doors and windows in the mews have a wire-covered frame which can be put in place when the window/door is opened. This helps prevent the ingress of vermin and also the escape of the inmates of the mews. All doors and windows are snug-fitting to help reduce draughts, which can be a killer for tethered hawks.

As accidents can happen at any time, it is common sense to also keep several fire extinguishers and a comprehensive first aid kit in the mews.

PERCHES

Whatever type of perch is used, the surface must be carefully considered. To be effective, the surface of the perch must be:

- Comfortable for the hawk
- Kind to the hawk's feet
- Easy to clean and maintain

On our shelf perches (see below), we use rubber matting, held in place by a piece of rubber inner tube. The rubber matting is removed, cleaned and replaced every day, to prevent the build-up of detritus and bacteria.

The blocks and bows we use are manufactured with heavy-duty pimpled rubber, which is kind to the hawk's feet and allows the circulation of air. The rubber is easy to clean and impervious to bacteria etc.

Some falconers utilise Astroturf for covering perches. While this material is adequate, we find that the base of the plastic 'grass' quickly fills with feathers, bits of food, etc., and this build-up is a perfect harbour for bacteria to breed, causing severe foot problems for the hawks which have to stand on the material day in and day out. If Astroturf is used, it must be thoroughly cleaned (no mean feat) every day, ensuring that material is not allowed to build up at the base of the stems of plastic grass.

I have also seen bow perches covered in rope. I find this unacceptably dangerous. It is all too easy for a hawk to snag a talon in the rope, and the talon will be ripped off, causing unnecessary suffering to the bird.

Although leather is sometimes used to cover perches, this material is totally unsuitable, as it easily absorbs water, mutes and blood, and becomes a perfect breeding ground for bacteria.

TYPES

Bow perch

Traditionally, hawks and buzzards have been provided with bow perches. As the name suggests, these are shaped like a bow, and have some form of 'padding' on the top part, on which the hawk can safely and comfortably perch. One can obtain bows which have spikes on each end, and are designed to be pushed into the ground. We prefer to use 'portable' bows; these have large, heavy feet on each end, and can be used on any surface. For large hawks, the feet should have a hole which can be used to peg the bow to prevent the hawk from moving it.

Block perch

Longwings have traditionally been supplied with block perches. These are round and have a large spike on the bottom to secure the perch to the ground. It is possible to buy portable blocks, but these can only be used for very small hawks, as they become too unwieldy and prone to toppling if made too large.

Shelf perch

The shelf perch is simply a semi-circular piece of wood, cut from a circle of 450 mm (18 inches), and mounted on the wall of the mews. It is important that the hawk cannot be left hanging, nor reach nearby hawks. Some falconers use a separate shelf, mounted 300 mm (12 inches) below the shelf perch, but we prefer to have our shelf perches a little lower to the ground, and thus do away with the necessity of these extra shelves. The leash and jesses must be of such a length that the hawk can jump onto the floor and then back onto the shelf perch, without being able to come into contact with nearby hawks.

Screen perch

The screen perch has killed too many hawks, and should not be used by any modern falconer who considers the welfare of the hawks of importance.

LEASHES, JESSES, ANKLETS AND SWIVELS

LEASHES

In order to secure the hawk to its perch, of whatever type, it is necessary to use a leash. There are three main types of leash – the 'traditional', the loop or button leash, and the 'hybrid' leash.

A hawk attached to the falconer's glove via a standard leash.

The traditional leash

This is simply a length of nylon rope (about 1 metre/39 inches) at the end of which a large knot is tied. A leather washer is slipped along the length of the rope to rest on the knot, as protection against fraying caused by the hawk bating and the leash rubbing on the perch ring to which the leash is attached. The ends of the rope need to be heat sealed, and coated with epoxy resin to prevent fraying. The leash needs to be fastened using the falconer's knot (see page 92). The problem with this type of leash is that the knot can work loose, either through the hawk's normal movements or through it deliberately attacking the knot. The result is an escaped hawk which, if tethered near other hawks, will almost certainly kill one or more before it makes good its escape.

The loop or button leash

This is about 400 mm (16 inches) long, with a loop at one end and a large button affixed at the other end. The loop end is threaded through the swivel (see photo on right) attached to the hawk's jesses, and then through the ring on the block or bow (perch). It then goes back to the swivel and through it, when the loop is passed over the button and the loop end fed back through the swivel. This gives a neat fastening on the securing ring of the block or bow. There is no knot to work loose, or for the hawk to unfasten. However, with a young hawk which is still inclined to bate, this type of leash can be difficult to release quickly enough, and the young hawk is liable to damage its feathers or worse. We use the traditional leash until such time as the hawk does not bate, but rather will step up on to the falconer's fist, at which time we change to the button leash.

A hawk attached to the falconer's glove via a standard leash.

The 'Hybrid' leash

This is a leash with a loop at one end, and a simple point on the other. It is fitted by threading the end of the leash through the swivel, and then through the leash's loop, thus securing it to the swivel. The end of the leash is secured to block, glove or vest with a falconer's knot.

'Bumper' leash

Where a bird bates a lot, and to help prevent damage to the hawk's legs, a 'bumper' leash can easily be made, simply by attaching a short (about 100-mm / four-inch) length of elastic between a loop of leash close to the swivel end. This will act as a form of shock absorber.

Leather should never be used for any leash of any type, as the material rapidly becomes hard and brittle, and is liable to break when the hawk bates.

JESSES AND ANKLETS

Jesses have been traditionally made from leather of one type or another. They can be fixed directly to the hawk's legs or, more usually today, fixed via anklets, or aylmeri to give them their correct name. Many UK falconers today use kangaroo skin for jesses and aylmeri, although many are using jesses manufactured from nylon. The modern idea is to use nylon jesses which are completely removed from the hawk before it is flown, while the hawk's aylmeri will have permanent jesses attached at all times, enabling the falconer to control the hawk when it returns to the fist.

With traditional jesses, one will need two sets – one set for use when tethering the hawk (mews jesses) and another set for fitting when flying the hawk (Flying jesses). Mews jesses have a slit in each to allow for fixing to a suitable swivel; such a slit would be dangerous for the hawk while it is being flown, as it could become caught on a branch. Flying jesses, therefore, have no slit.

SWIVELS

There are many types of swivels used by today's falconers, and some are, to say the least, downright dangerous (to the hawk). I recommend that one uses only the best swivels made by and for falconers. I have seen falconers use dog swivels and catches, fishing swivels and all kinds of rubbish. Why? If a swivel fails, the result is a lost hawk, and possibly one or more other hawks killed by the hawk before it leaves the weathering. I have even met falconers who cannot/will not tie the falconer's knot, and who simply 'secure' their hawks by using a catch similar to that used on a dog's lead. Such items should not be considered by any falconer except for specialist usage and, even then, must be treated with the utmost care, being inspected on a daily basis. These catches are prone to damage and failure – a hawk which becomes free in a mews housing several other hawks, will inevitably attack and kill the tethered birds.

HOODING

A hood is used to keep a hawk calm, and is simply a method of 'blindfolding'. With longwings, hooding is considered to be an essential part of the basic training, but hoods are also used with both broadwings and shortwings. The idea of the hood is simple – to keep the hawk calm when it is being manned, when it is travelling, and while being carried – either on the fist or on a cadge. Where one or more hawks are being carried, the hood comes into its own, and particularly so when another hawk is being flown.

The hood has two pairs of braces, traditionally made from leather, but now often made from Gortex: one pair is long and has pointed ends, while the other pair is short and has knots in the ends. To 'draw' (i.e. close) the hood, the long pair is pulled, using one's ungloved hand and one's teeth, and to 'strike' (i.e. open) the hood, the shorter pair is pulled, again using the ungloved hand and teeth. On the top of the hood is a knot (a 'top knot'), made from a Turk's head knot of leather which acts as a handle, allowing the hood to be placed on the hawk's head, or removed. Some hoods

A group of students on a Lantra 'Beginning Falconry' course, held at the
National Falconry School. (*Photo: Nick Ridley*)

(particularly Dutch hoods) have a plume of feathers attached to this top knot: these
feathers are traditionally those of the hawk's favoured quarry.

The hood must be a precise piece of equipment if it is to do its job properly. A badly
fitting hood may allow the hawk to see or to shrug off the hood (if it is too large),
while a hood which is too small may damage the hawk's eyes and will always make
the hawk so uncomfortable that it may become hood shy – a state of affairs where
the hawk will not easily take to being hooded, with all the consequent stress that this
involves. In particular, the beak opening must be of the correct size: too large and the
hawk will be able to see the outside world, too small and the hawk will not be able
to cast, and may choke to death.

There are three main types of hood available to the modern falconer, although
there are numerous variations on these styles:

1. Anglo-Indian hood
2. Bahraini hood
3. Dutch hood

The Anglo-Indian hood

Made from a single piece of leather, the Anglo-Indian hood is used widely by many falconers, especially when first making a hawk to the hood.

The Bahraini hood

Again, made from a single piece of leather, and particularly good for accipiters, the Bahraini hood is favoured by Arab falconers, particularly for use on sakers and peregrines, but it is also used on many other types of longwings. Unlike the Anglo-Indian hood, which has an open back, the Bahraini hood has a concertinaed back.

The Dutch Hood

Unlike the other two types above, the Dutch hood is made from three separate pieces of leather – two sides and a top/back piece – and the hoods are blocked, i.e. the leather used is soaked in water and, while still wet, placed on a block of wood, shaped in the image of the hawk's head, and then smoothed into the exact shape of the block. Traditionally, the side panels of the Dutch hood are a different colour from the top. Some falconers have intricate designs or even paintings of their hawk put on the side panels.

WHICH SPECIES NEED HOODING

Traditionally, only longwings and eagles have been hooded on a regular basis, but there is great advantage in making to the hood every hawk, even Harris' hawks. The reason for this is obvious: when hooded, it is far easier and less stressful – for both hawk and falconer – when fitting furniture, coping or imping. For this reason, we here at the National Falconry School, ensure that every hawk is made to the hood during early manning.

OBTAINING A HOOD

Whilst it is possible to make a hood, to make a *good* hood is extremely difficult, and it is true to say that most modern falconers choose to purchase a hood from a trusted source (see Appendix 3 Useful Organisations at the end of this book).

If the reader wishes to attempt such a project, I would recommend starting with an Anglo-Indian hood; patterns for these hoods are widely available in many falconry books, such as *Falconry Art and Practice* by Emma Ford.

HOW TO HOOD A HAWK

After selecting a suitable hood, have the hawk sitting comfortably on the fist, with the hood held (by the top knot) in the opposite hand, out of sight of the hawk. Still holding the hood by the top knot, with the beak opening pointing downwards and the inside of the hood pointing at the hawk, slowly raise the hood towards the hawk's head and place it, in a circular motion, over the hawk's head, taking great care not to move the gloved fist. Draw the braces, using the free hand and one's teeth in a smooth motion, ensuring that no sideways pressure is applied to the hawk's head or neck. If the hawk bates, continue to hood it, holding it across the knee and placing the hood on its head. With practice, it is possible to draw the hood with one hand. Once the hood is firmly in place, the hawk can be lifted onto the fist, where it should quickly settle down.

To my mind, it is far better to hood a difficult hawk in this manner than to try and do battle with it. Such action will instil in the hawk that the hood is nasty and something to be avoided (this is known as negative reinforcement).

MOULTING

During their day-to-day actions, hawks (as with all birds, both in the wild and in captivity) will damage their feathers. While these can be repaired (See Imping, below), it is natural for the hawk to moult, i.e. shed old feathers and grow new ones. During the moult, it is imperative that the hawk gets plenty of top quality feed, giving it a good, balanced diet.

During the moult, and also during the breeding season, we feed our hawks a three-day rotational diet of day-old chicks, rodents (mice, rats, hamsters, etc.), and quail. At regular intervals, we add measured amounts (dependent on species and gender) of specialist avian multi-vitamin and mineral supplement, to ensure that the hawks get all the nutrition they require.

Where feed and nutrients are insufficient, deformities (referred to as 'fret lines') will appear on the hawk's feathers.

IMPING

When a hawk's feathers are bent, they can easily be straightened by the application of heat. This heat can be applied via steam or by using a specialist feather straightener, which is heated in very hot water, and then applied to the bent feather. When the hawk's 'train' (tail) is bent, it may be dipped in warm water which will help straighten it. This procedure should not be carried out too often, as the dipping will remove much of the oil in the hawk's feathers, making them brittle and prone to breaking.

When a flight feather is broken (i.e. wing or tail primary, or secondary feathers), it will affect the hawk's flight, and so it should be repaired by imping, a skill in which every falconer must become competent, as it is a task which will be necessary during every season in which a hawk is flown to quarry.

During the moult, every intact primary and secondary feather should be collected, cleaned and dried, and then placed in an airtight 'feather box': these feathers will be used for imping purposes.

When selecting a feather for imping use, select one that is the same size or bigger (it is possible to trim an over-sized feather), and preferably from the same species, or even the same hawk. Also, ensure that the feather is from the same side of the train or wing.

Gather together all necessary equipment:

- Suitable feather
- Imping needles
- Glue
- Scalpel
- Cutting mat
- Card

Once all the equipment has been gathered, hood and cast the hawk (see below), and have an assistant hold it firmly but softly, on its breast, with the relevant wing or train uncovered. The broken feather to be imped should next be isolated from the surrounding feathers by placing a piece of card under the relevant feather, and over the surrounding feathers.

Where the feather is broken near the base, the repair is known as basal imping, and should be repaired in the following manner. Cut the broken feather at the base, where the webbing of the feather begins, ensuring that you have left a good stub into which the replacement feather will be imped. Next cut the replacement feather to the correct length, i.e. so that it lines up with the surrounding feathers. Next, one will need an imping needle, and this can be a piece of bamboo, a steel rod or needle, or a piece of carbon fibre rod. In the past I have used needles, and would always choose a leather-working needle which is triangular in profile. Never use a rounded imping needle as this will not adhere properly to the inside of the feather's shaft. With bamboo and carbon fibre, it is necessary to file flat at least two sides or make an oval shape from the material. The length of the imping needle should be ample to fit in both pieces of feather, and this will vary from species to species, between the sexes, and also between individual hawks.

Test the imping needle for a tight fit in first one and then the other feather shaft: if a needle is too tight, and it is forced into the shaft, the shaft will split. Where the base feather shaft is split, repair is almost always impossible, and so great care should be taken in this matter.

Once one has determined that the feather is the correct length, and the imping needle fits both ends of the feathers to be used, glue should be placed on each end of the needle, and one end pushed firmly into place in the replacement feather. I will not use super glue for this task, as I always seem to end up with the feather and needle stuck to me. I prefer to use a contact adhesive, which needs to be applied and then left for a couple of minutes to begin curing, before it is inserted into the ends of the feathers. If care has been taken in measuring the feathers and imping needle, once the two ends are joined, the joint should be almost invisible to the human eye. Always ensure that the feather is positioned in the correct plane, and in line with the surrounding feathers before the glue has time to set. Any excess glue should be wiped off as soon as the joint has been made successfully. The needle forms the centre of the repair and remains in the feather.

Sometimes, the break is not low down on the feather, and this can be repaired by what is known as needle imping; the only difference is that extremely fine sewing needles, designed for leather working (i.e. with a triangular profile), are used.

CASTING A HAWK

When carrying out work on a hawk, it is necessary to immobilise it for its own and the falconer's protection, and this is done by casting the hawk.

With an unmanned hawk, the bird is caught and held by the ankles, and then lowered onto a towel placed on a large piece of thick foam rubber. As it is placed on the towel, its wings should be carefully closed by an assistant, and then the towel wrapped around it, holding its wings closed, and covering its head, until the hawk's hood can be fitted. The towel should be wrapped firmly but loosely, ensuring that the hawk is secured within its folds. The towel will protect the hawk's feathers from damage while the falconer works. Commercially made devices, somewhat resembling straight-jackets, and secured by Velcro tabs, are available and make the job of casting a hawk much simpler.

With a manned hawk, the procedure is similar, except that the hawk is held on the fist and hooded, at which time the assistant will place a towel around it from the rear of the hawk.

When the hawk is secured, it can be placed on its breast for imping and coping, or on its back for aylmeri/jess fitting. When on its breast, the hawk's feet will be pushed into the foam rubber cushion, which they will grip, thus preventing it from piercing its foot with its own talons. Whenever a hawk is cast, it must be held softly but firmly by an assistant, using wide spread hands to hold it in place. Never make the mistake of believing that a cast hawk will not attempt to break free – it will, and if it succeeds in escaping the consequences could be fatal.

When fitting aylmeri/jesses, the assistant must securely hold both of the hawk's legs while the falconer fits the furniture. All furniture to be fitted must be pre-made and greased, with all necessary equipment laid to hand for the falconer. Holding a cast hawk for 10 to 15 minutes while the necessary furniture and equipment is gathered, is not good practice.

COPING

All captive hawks will require both their talons and their beaks to be trimmed to length and filed into shape; this is known as coping.

I am often asked why this state of affairs does not exist in the wild, i.e. why don't wild hawks get overgrown talons and/or beaks? In the wild, a hawk would normally keep its beak and talons in trim by the constant wear on them of the bones of its prey, and would regularly feak (i.e. wipe its beak) on favoured, abrasive rocks. However, even this will not protect a hawk indefinitely from having an overgrown beak or talons. Some falconers will insist that it is the diet of captive hawks which makes them susceptible to long beaks and talons – this is not wholly correct. I fly a cast of Harris' hawks, which are siblings. Both are treated in the same manner and fed on the same feed. One requires coping every year, whilst the other can go for two or more years without the necessity of coping either beak or talons. However, as a falconer, one must accept that coping is a skill which must be mastered and which will need to be practised regularly, in order to keep one's hawks in top condition, especially as even the 'best' hawk can accidentally crack its beak on a bone.

A male Harris' hawk with an overgrown beak requiring coping.

As a matter of course, we always cope both beak and talons when we put a hawk for moulting, and always cope talons on every hawk when we first take it up for training. The latter is important, as it helps prevent a nervous hawk from grabbing itself and doing injury. A newly taken-up hawk will often clench its feet, piercing its own foot, and this will almost inevitably lead to an infection (see 'Bumblefoot', Chapter 9).

TOOLS

The tools necessary for coping a hawk need to be at hand before the hawk is cast, and consist of:

- Cutters
- Small files
- Styptic pencil

Cutters

The cutters may be traditional side cutters, such as are used for cutting human toe nails, or the type of cutters sold for trimming the claws of dogs – I favour the latter.

Using the cutters, the point of the beak should be trimmed to length. As this varies from bird to bird, it is advised that, for the first few times this exercise is undertaken, guidance from an experienced falconer should be sought and acted on. If cut too short, the beak will bleed and obviously cause pain/discomfort to the hawk. Where bleeding does occur, it should be stemmed by the use of a styptic pencil, which will need to be held in place for several minutes, to allow it to do its job.

Small files

Once cut to length, the beak should be filed into shape using a selection of small files. I recommend that one file should be broad and flat, one with a slight curve and one square: this will cover all aspects of a hawk's beak, be it a falcon, a hawk or an eagle. The size of the files needed is obviously dependent upon the species being coped.

Talons will also need cutting to length, and then filing smooth, to remove the possibility of splits, which will be painful to the hawk.

Stypic pencil

While it is obviously hoped that one will not be necessary (it is to stem blood flow if the beak and/or talons are cut too short), it is a wise precaution to have a styptic pencil to hand.

Under no circumstance should scissors be used for trimming talons. Scissors work in a way which may result in the talon being ripped, especially if the hawk moves a foot during the trimming operation.

FEED INFLUENCE ON FREQUENCY OF NEED TO COPE

By feeding hard bones to the hawk on a regular basis, one may reduce the need to cope her beak too often, but this does not always work. It is also possible for a hawk to damage – split or crack – its beak on a hard bone. We regularly feed rabbit feet and heads to our larger hawks, and find it beneficial. The hawks seem to welcome the challenge of these objects, referred to as tirings.

RANGLE

Rangle is a natural way that wild hawks have of cleaning their stomach, and consists of small, rounded stones or pebbles. In captivity, most hawks are deprived of the opportunity to avail themselves of rangle, and so it is down to the falconer to provide this.

Some falconers will never give rangle, while others will give it to their hawks on a regular basis. Some falconers feel that rangle is, at best, useless, and at worst potentially lethal, and yet many experienced falconers will praise the effects of rangle on a hawk.

If one decides that rangle is useful for the hawk (and I believe it is), then it is best given when the hawk has been taken up from its aviary, either for the first time or after moulting, and has lost weight to a degree whereby it is ready for the creance; at this stage, we feed meat without castings. Wait until the crop has been put-over (i.e. emptied by the hawk), which will usually be late evening. With some hawks, simply putting the rangle on the floor in front of them will be all that is needed, while with others it will be necessary to hood the bird, and then place the rangle – piece by piece – in the mouth. We repeat this procedure every night for between seven and ten days.

The rangle works by cleaning out the lining of the stomach, and this appears to have a beneficial effect on the condition and fitness of the hawk.

ASSESSING THE HEALTH AND CONDITION OF HAWKS

> It is essential that the falconer constantly assesses the condition and fitness of all hawks kept by him, and this should be done by a combination of the following:
>
> • Weighing
> • Feeling the keel and muscles of the hawk's chest
> • Observation of the hawk's flying and general behaviour

WEIGHING

We weigh our flying hawks (not aviary hawks) on a regular, daily basis, at or as near to the same time of day as possible. All the weights are recorded on a large whiteboard on the wall in the mews. This gives all our falconers, at a glance, vital information concerning each hawk's weight for the last seven days.

We weigh all the hawks with their jesses, leashes, hoods, etc. While some falconers will remove one or more of these items prior to weighing the hawks, as long as the items are consistent, such matters do not affect the weighing of the hawk.

FEELING THE HAWK'S CHEST

Feeling the keel (breast bone) allows you to assess how much fat is around this bone. By carrying out this procedure on a daily basis, in conjunction with weighing, the falconer will have a realistic view of the hawk's condition.

OBSERVATION

A hawk straight from the aviary will be fat and fairly fit; at this time the hawk is also

A Bengal eagle owl (*Bubo bengalensis*), a medium-sized owl popular with many owl keepers.

very strong, and may well struggle fiercely when restrained or cast. It will, however, become breathless very quickly, and will be lethargic and slow in its responses to the falconer, lure etc. If a fat, fit bird is flown at the lure or quarry, it may well overfly or even ignore these, and even refuse to feed on the fist, bating or even refusing to stand on the fist.

A fit hawk will sit on the fist, not bate (provided it has been properly manned), happily and enthusiastically chase its quarry or the lure, and eat its feed with great exuberance and even impatience. When resting, such a hawk will sit with feathers fluffed up, one leg raised, and (if a longwing) its wings crossed over the top of its train (tail).

A hawk in low condition will not fly very strongly and tire easily, often leading to it giving up the chase on quarry or pitching (landing) when flown to the lure. Such a hawk will grab at its food and take one or two quick bites, but then stand holding it without eating, for some time. When it sits on the block, it may sit on both feet, or on one foot and the knuckle of the other, and its wings may well droop below its train. If it has the strength to bate, such bating will be obviously weak.

If a hawk is seen to be on its block, standing on both feet, feathers fluffed and eyes half-closed, and generally seems uncoordinated, it is in a very low condition and extremely close to death.

TRANSPORTING HAWKS

It will always be necessary, at some stage, to transport the hawk, whether this be to the hunting ground, a show or the vet's surgery, and this transport needs to be carried out with the health and safety of all concerned – hawks, humans, dogs, etc. – first and foremost in everyone's consideration.

I have seen some falconers who seem to delight in the attention that a hawk brings them, and these people will happily sit their hawk on the back of a car seat while making fairly long journeys. I can only condemn such people as foolish, inconsiderate and not worthy of the title of falconer. A hawk carried in such a manner can easily bate off its 'perch', and cause the driver to lose concentration, which may lead to a serious accident and even the death of one or more people – not to mention the hawk.

HAWK BOXES

We use specially constructed hawk carry boxes, with different sizes and shapes being used for different species. Whatever design you use, the box should hold the hawk securely, even when the door is opened, be well ventilated without letting in light, be comfortable for the occupant, and have a secure perch on which the hawk can sit without any damage to its train, head or wing tips.

CADGES

The old-fashioned method of transporting hawks was a cadge, which resembles a coffee table on which the maker has forgotten to place a top. The modern cadge comes in two styles: the box cadge for transporting the hawk(s) while in a vehicle (it has solid sides, allowing the hawk to brace its tail against the sides when the vehicle is moving), and the field cadge for carrying the hawks in the field. Some falconers have taken the design of each and combined them, resulting in a field cadge which fits in a box, making it a box cadge.

The tops of the cadges are covered in carpet or padded leather (where the hawks sit), and have a metal loop to which the hawks' leashes can be tied. The leash has to be shortened considerably to ensure that the hawks cannot move too much. It is best if they have only the length of their jesses to move.

Hawks carried on cadges should never be left unattended.

DAILY ROUTINE

I am a big believer in the importance of a set routine to ensure that all tasks are carried out properly. Here at The National Falconry School, our day begins with checking that all the birds are safe and well. This is carried out via a visual check of our mews birds and then our aviary birds. Any hawk which does not seem 100% is physically examined and, if necessary, treated accordingly.

Once all the birds have been checked, the mews hawks are taken outside and tethered on the weathering ground. If the weather is severely inclement, we put the hawks under a large barn, where they will receive protection from the elements. On the weathering, the hawks are tethered to a freshly cleaned bow or block perch (dependent on the species of hawk), and given access to a bath of fresh, clean water. If the ambient temperature is fairly high, we will also spray the hawks, using a hose pipe adjusted to give a soft spray. This spraying helps keep the hawks clean and their feathers in good condition. Once the feathers have dried, the hawk will begin preening, i.e. cleaning and grooming its feathers. At such times, the hawk will use its beak to squeeze a light oil from its preen gland, which is situated at the base of the tail. The hawk will then anoint its feathers with this oil, thus making them more waterproof. By being left on the weathering, the hawks also get the opportunity to sun-bathe, and this is vitally important to their health and well-being. Sunshine contains ultraviolet rays, and these rays act on provitamin S, contained in the oil from the preen gland, to produce vitamin D_3. Vitamin D_3 is essential for the absorption of calcium, an essential element in the growth of bones and feathers.

While the hawks are weathering, we clean out the mews, using scrapers and a power hose. Once all of the physical detritus has been removed, we spray with a suitable disinfectant and then rinse the surfaces with clean water. Once the mews are dry, we place a sheet of newspaper under every shelf perch. This paper will catch

Harris' hawks on the weathering. Note the rubber-topped bow perches. *(Photo: Nick Ridley)*

the mutes and also the casts, helping us ensure that every hawk has cast before it is weighed.

During the summer months, if the weather is extremely hot, we will put out the hawks as usual in the morning, and take them under cover, or return them to the cooler mews, in the heat of the afternoon.

Our weathering is surrounded by a high chain-link fence, but we never leave the hawks unattended, as the danger of attack from foxes, stray dogs, or even some misguided humans, is ever present.

Later in the day, we will return the birds to their mews, where they will be weighed, and their weight/condition noted on a large whiteboard; we then fly each hawk in turn. With some hawks, it is easy to fly them in a cast (i.e. two together); with Harris'hawks, we often fly/exercise up to six hawks at the same time. Never try flying a hawk with others still tethered on the weathering, as this is asking for trouble, and will inevitably lead to the injury or death of the tethered hawk(s).

In summer, once all the hawks have been exercised and fed the appropriate amount and type of food for the day, we return them all to the weathering until early evening, at which time the hawks are returned to the mews. In the short winter days, we are unable to give the hawks this extra weathering time.

We always check all hawks last thing at night.

CHAPTER 4

TRAINING

The training of hawks varies from species to species, and this chapter gives general information, while the specifics for the three sections into which hawks are divided, i.e. shortwings, broadwings and longwings, are given if they vary from the general information given.

MANNING

Without a doubt, proper manning is the most important aspect of the training of all hawks. Manning is the foundation on which all other training will rest. Poorly manned hawks will never settle to their work, and the falconer with a poorly manned hawk will rue the fact that he did not spend more time on this important aspect of hawk training.

When a hawk is first taken up from the aviary, it will be at its heaviest, i.e. its 'top weight', and with shortwings and broadwings, will not tolerate the falconer. Such hawks need to have their weight reduced before real manning is started.

The traditional / classic method of commencing manning is to assess the hawk's condition when it is first taken up, after which it is hooded and then the falconer and his assistant must fit the hawk's furniture. The properly equipped and hooded hawk is then taken into a darkened and silent room, where the falconer will sit the hawk on his fist (while it is still hooded). While this can take a few minutes and definitely requires the falconer to show patience, it is a fairly easy procedure. Once the hawk is comfortably sitting on the falconer's fist, the falconer must carefully and slowly loosen the hood's braces (straps), pausing whenever the hawk becomes too agitated. Once the hood is loose, the hawk should be left sitting on the falconer's fist for about twenty to thirty seconds, after which time the falconer will remove the hood completely. As this is done, the hawk will almost certainly fling itself off the falconer's fist (referred to as bating). Because of this, the falconer should take great care to ensure that the hawk is held securely (we always tie the hawk's leash to the ring on the gauntlet before commencing any work with a hawk), and well away from any solid objects (tables, chairs, etc.) on which it could injure itself.

When the hawk bates, the falconer must lift it back onto the glove with his free

The author's son, Tom, a falconer from a very early age, holding a mature male Harris' hawk (*Parabuteo unicinctus*). Note that the hawk is securely attached to the falconer's hawking vest. This is best practice, and only a fool would carry a hawk on its mews jesses, swivel and leash without having it secured to his person.

hand, either by placing his hand under its chest, or on its back. When lifting an unmanned hawk by her chest, it is not unusual for the falconer's hand to be bitten by the hawk, and so a falconer will often wear a lightweight leather glove, to protect his hand from the hawk's bite.

Once the hawk is back on the fist, it will usually bate again, and so the process must be repeated until such time as the hawk sits – at first for only a few seconds – on the falconer's fist. It is important that, throughout this process, the falconer keeps extremely still and quiet, and gives the hawk his full concentration.

All such manning sessions should be of only a short duration: a maximum of thirty minutes is recommended. It is possible to put in two or three such sessions in a day, with a couple of hours respite being given to the hawk between each session, to prevent it becoming too tired and stressed.

About ten years ago, staff here at The National Falconry School tried a new tactic with all of our new/young hawks, which has been extremely successful for us, allowing us to train our birds more quickly, easily and effectively, and also with far less stress for everyone concerned – humans and hawks. Once we have taken up the hawks from the aviary, we fit their furniture, and a hood, and assess their condition, before weighing them. The assessment of a hawk's condition should be carried out by feeling the keel (breast bone), and assessing how much fat is around this bone. To a beginner, this is almost impossible but, by carrying out the assessment on a daily basis while the hawk's rations are reduced, the tyro will soon begin to appreciate the subtleties of this method. When used in conjunction with weighing, the falconer will have a realistic view of the hawk's condition at any time. When a novice falconer (an apprentice) is guided by a seasoned and highly experienced falconer (a master falconer), such methods can be described and practised by the apprentice without risk to the hawk.

Once our new hawks have been assessed, we take them to a secluded weathering lawn, away from the main thoroughfares within the School's grounds, and there we block them, i.e. tether them to blocks (for longwings) or bow perches (broadwings and accipiters). Once secured to the blocks, we leave the hood on each hawk and leave the hawks on the weathering lawn until later in the day. Our weathering lawn is well shaded, and thus the hawks are not subjected to direct sunlight with its inherent dangers of heat and sunstroke. Were this not the case, we would supply each hawk with a sunshade, parasol or similar, and ensure that it was moved throughout the day to provide shade for the hawks.

When the hawks are returned to their mews, we cover the floor with carpet, to prevent the hawks from damaging their feathers during the inevitable bates which will occur as a result of the hawks not yet being used to their jesses restricting their movements. The hawks are unhooded when tethered to their perch in the mews.

After a couple of days of this, we find that the hawks are much easier to handle, and more accepting of humans, even if only at a distance initially. At this stage, we block the birds, but remove each hawk's hood, before leaving the hawks tethered on the weathering lawn.

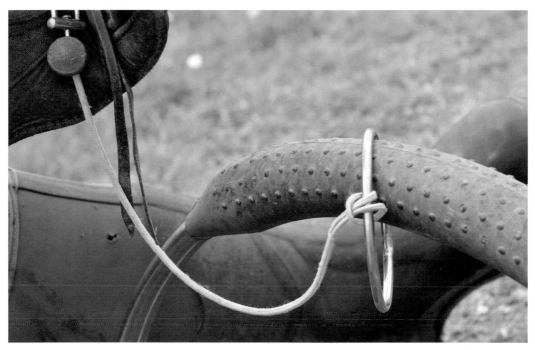

A button leash attaching a Harris' hawk to a bow perch. Note that there is no knot for the hawk to unfasten, and that the length of the leash will never vary.

At the start and end of each day, the condition of each hawk is again assessed and, once the hawks' weight is down to a level where we feel that the hawk will be more receptive to us, we commence proper manning.

By using this method, we have found that the hawks quickly become calmer and more accepting of humans, thus helping us with our manning process and reducing the stress levels for all concerned.

As mentioned earlier in this chapter, a shortwing will not be able to be manned directly from its top weight, and so the hawk's condition must be assessed and its weight reduced to a level whereby it can be manned.

Once the hawk has learned to sit on the falconer's fist, even if only for a few seconds, it should be offered food, which will be held in the falconer's gloved fist – feeding off the fist for the first time is a milestone in training. As to how quickly a hawk will bend its neck to reach and thus eat the proffered feed is dependent on both the skill of the falconer and on the hunger of the hawk. The falconer must learn how to wriggle the proffered food in just the right way to attract the hungry hawk. While some hawks will take the food quite easily and early in their training, others are more stubborn, and it is by no means unknown for such a stubborn hawk to go several days without taking food. It is obviously imperative that the hawk is not fed in the mews, but that the falconer keeps his nerve and only offers food to the hawk when the hawk is on the falconer's fist. If a hawk is fed in the mews, it will have no reason to feed on the fist.

As the time spent on trying to get the hawk to feed on the falconer's fist progresses, the bird's attention will be centred on the food and whether or not to eat, and it will forget about thinking of escaping from the falconer's fist. As such, the hawk will become steadier on the fist as every training session goes by, and its bating will happen less often. If the falconer can put in a few sessions, it is possible to get the hawk to willingly sit on the scales of its own accord, without bating, within the first 24 to 36 hours of the commencement of training. It is from the daily weighing, and the weights recorded, that the hawk's flying weight will be found and, as such, it is important that the hawk is weighed at the same time each day, ensuring that the hawk has no food in its guts, thus giving an accurate picture of the hawk's condition. These weights should be recorded assiduously by the falconer. We have over twenty birds which we fly on a daily basis here at The National Falconry School, and we record all of the weights of each hawk on a large whiteboard which is affixed to the wall in the mews, adjacent to the scales. For a falconer with only one or two hawks, a notebook will suffice and, when still a novice, the falconer is advised to note everything of consequence regarding the hawk and its training. Such information will be priceless to the tyro as he progresses through his falconry career.

Even when the bird is trained and used for hunting, it is still advisable to keep accurate records of weights, performance and other factors which will impact on the training and feed given to the hawk. Even variables such as the weather should be recorded, as these have an effect on the amount of food which the hawk requires to keep at peak fitness. All birds, like mammals, are homoeothermic, and use stored energy and food to maintain their optimum body temperature. Obviously, in very cold conditions, more food (energy) will be required than in warm periods.

While some books give detailed charts of the 'optimum weight' for each hawk, I believe that such information is, at best, misleading and, at worst, potentially fatal to the hawk concerned. There are great variations between sexes, species and, of course, individual hawks, and it is impossible to give any table of weights which would be worth reading. While some hawks will need to lose 20% of their body weight to achieve their flying weight, others will not, and for the novice falconer to simply drop the hawk's weight by this amount may all too easily end up with a dead hawk. It is by far a better practice to drop the hawk's weight in small degrees while at the same time assessing the hawk's condition on a daily basis.

Once the falconer has got the hawk to a level whereby it will enthusiastically feed off the fist whenever food is presented, it is time for the falconer to begin walking around the weathering lawn and other such places (which should still be fairly quiet and out-of-the-way) with the hawk on his fist. By doing so, the hawk will become more used to the antics of Man and his machines, the environment in general, and the presence of other humans, dogs and hawks. During all such excursions, the hawk must be securely fastened to the falconer's glove, and the hawk should be given food, in the form of a tiring, during these outings, especially when there is something which the hawk has not seen before and which it may take as potentially dangerous. At such times, the falconer should stop, stand still and encourage the hawk to feed. By doing this, the hawk will quickly come to accept these incidents for what they are – daily occurrences which offer no danger whatsoever to the hawk. Staff here try to ensure that the hawk is introduced to a new experience on every outing, and under strictly controlled conditions, e.g. a hawk will be carried towards a vehicle, parked but with its engine running. The next time, the vehicle will move off away from the falconer and his charge, and the time after, the vehicle will move off towards the falconer and his hawk. By managing the situations and steadily increasing the severity while still maintaining full control, it is possible to introduce a young hawk to all manner of new experiences. The aim, by the end of formal manning, is to have the hawk steady to almost everything that it will meet, from dogs to noisy children, flapping flags to moving lorries. Remember, that for the young hawk, what to you is a common-place event, may well be quite intimidating and even frightening. The more time put in on manning a young hawk, the better adult it will grow to be.

Unlike shortwings and broadwings, the falconer can start training a longwing to sit on and feed off the fist almost as soon as the hawk is taken from the aviary, without the necessity to reduce the hawk's weight first. From that stage, the falconer should continue as detailed above.

TRAINING

STEPPING UP

The next stage for a young hawk is to persuade it to step off its perch and onto the falconer's gloved fist, with food again being the driving force; this is referred to as 'stepping up'.

As soon as the young hawk is confidently eating off the fist (usually within a day or so of first feeding off the fist), and assuming it is kept in its own weathering or mews, the falconer should approach the young hawk (which will be tethered to its block at this stage) and pick it up onto the fist. It is highly likely that, as the falconer attempts this manoeuvre, the hawk will bate away from him. If this happens, the falconer must quickly scoop up the hawk and place it on his fist, where the hawk will find a tempting morsel of food, which the falconer will be holding tightly between thumb and finger. By doing this gently, and then standing still for a few seconds to let the hawk get its feet, the hawk should start to feed. After allowing the hawk one or two bites of the food, the falconer should then replace the hawk on the block, while lifting the hawk's train (tail) with his right hand, ungloved, thus encouraging the hawk to step backwards onto the block. Immediately the hawk is sitting on the block, the falconer should place his gloved hand, still holding the food, in front of the hawk, with the food being slightly higher than the hawk's feet, and the hand just far enough in front of the hawk to allow the hawk to just reach the food. As it reaches for the food, grabbing it and trying to bite off a piece, the falconer should raise his hand slightly, taking the food just out of reach of the hawk, preventing it from taking a piece of the meat. The hawk will become irritated by the inability to feed, and will strike at the glove with one foot, in an effort to hold the glove, and therefore the meat, in a position where it can reach and therefore eat the meat. As the hawk grabs the glove, the falconer should gently but firmly raise the gloved hand, making the hawk lift its other foot on to the glove and thus stepping up onto the fist and off the block.

This stepping up marks another landmark in the young hawk's training, and will make the action of taking up the hawk from the block much easier in future, as the falconer can tempt it to step on to his fist by holding a piece of meat between finger and thumb. This piece of meat is referred to as a 'pick-up piece', and can be used over the next few days or even weeks to ensure that the hawk associates being taken up by the falconer with a pleasurable experience, i.e. being fed.

JUMPING

Once the young hawk will happily step up onto the falconer's fist for the pick-up piece, it is time to put the next link of the learning chain in place – getting the hawk to jump a short distance onto the falconer's fist, again for a reward of food. With many hawks, it is possible to move on to this next step on the same day that it has been taught to step-up. The piece of meat used for this exercise must be much bigger and hence far more tempting for the hawk, than that used in the earlier stepping-up exercise; we tend to use a full day-old chick or a quail leg.

The falconer should start the exercise by getting the hawk to step-up for one bite of meat, unfasten its leash from the block and affix it securely to his glove, and then replace the hawk on the block. He should then place his hand slightly further away from the hawk, just a few centimetres, so that the hawk cannot just step across the gap, and onto the falconer's glove. When the hawk realises that the food is just too far away for a step, it will crane its neck, bend forwards and do just about anything other than take that first initial jump onto the falconer's fist. It may even manage to grab the glove with one foot and then step-up to take a bite of the food, but it must not be allowed to take more than one small bite before being returned to the block.

To persuade the hawk to carry out the exercise, and also to condition it for future training, the falconer should call to it. We use both a visible and an audible signal to the hawk: we tap the food on the glove with the fingers of the right (ungloved) hand, while at the same time giving a whistle. While some falconers will use a stag horn or even a referee's whistle, we prefer to whistle with our lips only. It is all too easy to lose a stag horn whistle, but impossible to lose one's lips.

Eventually, and often out of sheer frustration, the hawk will jump onto the fist, at which time it must be rewarded by allowing it to take a couple of good bites of the proffered food, after which stage it is returned to its block. Once it has managed a jump, the hawk usually gets the message and will happily jump to the glove each time it is proffered. The exercise should be repeated several times before adding yet another link to the hawk's learning chain.

This next link is added by simply increasing the distance that the hawk will be asked to jump, eventually jumping the full length of the leash (about a metre). Once it will do this, the exercise is varied and extended by taking the hawk outside, and then starting again from the step-up exercise. While this may seem needlessly repetitive, it should be remembered that, to this stage, the hawk has not been subjected to all of the distractions that will face it in the outside world as it has been trained within the sheltered confines of the weathering or mews. Once it is outside, and there are many distractions, it may well need encouragement to simply step up. However, with patience, repetition and rewards, it should soon be jumping the length of the leash from its block on the weathering lawn to the falconer's glove, ignoring all the distractions that will inevitably be in the outside world. It is highly unlikely that this will be achieved on the same day as the other goals already achieved; it may even be necessary to start from scratch and train it again to take food from the falconer's fist. Often, a further slight reduction in the hawk's weight is necessary to get it to overcome its fear of performing in the open air. Patience is always needed if all of the good work already carried out is not to be wasted.

USING THE CREANCE

The word 'creance' is a French term used in financial dealings, and which means to get a return. In falconry, a creance (a length of string) is used to ensure that a falconer's young (and as yet untrained) hawk returns during the training sessions.

Before starting work on the creance, the hawk must willingly and easily step-up and jump the length of the leash outside in the open air, and a few minutes should be spent on these exercises before the leash is exchanged for the creance. The area chosen for creance training must also be given some careful consideration; it should be a smooth area, with the grass cut very short and containing nothing on which the creance may snag.

Once the creance is fitted securely to the young hawk, and the other end is securely tied so as to ensure that the hawk cannot fly off on its own, it should be placed on a block and called increasing distances to the falconer's glove, where it can plainly see food. The first flight should be about 1½ to 2 metres, and if the hawk's weight has been managed correctly, it should jump/fly this distance immediately it is shown the food. While some falconers will ask the hawk to come three or four times this distance from the start, I prefer to begin with small flights and then gradually build up to longer ones. When the hawk is asked to perform long flights from the start, it will often refuse to do so until it feels ready – by doing this the hawk is training the falconer and thereby developing an extremely bad habit. If a distance is reached at which the hawk hesitates, then the falconer should give an audible signal (we use a

Training the hawk on a creance. Once the session is completed, the falconer must wind the creance on its stick, in such a manner as to ensure it will not tangle, and using only one hand.

whistle, as detailed earlier) in combination with the visual signal. If the hawk still refuses to come to the falconer's fist, the distance should be reduced and the hawk called again. A hawk which behaves like this will require a slight reduction in food, and thus in weight.

The action of asking the hawk to leave its block or any perch and fly to the falconer's fist is referred to as 'calling off'.

Once the hawk is given creance training, all of its food should be fed to it during the training sessions, a small bite at a time, as a reward for carrying out the actions required.

The objective of creance training is to get the hawk to fly the full length of the creance immediately it is called, and to do this, it may be necessary to further reduce the hawk's weight a little at a time, until it is sharp enough to fly to the falconer's fist as soon as it is presented with food on the glove. There are, however, exceptions to this, and we have had many hawks which, when at the creance training stage, will fly to the falconer before he has had the chance to place it on the block and walk the length of the creance. When this happens, the falconer should enlist the help of an assistant, who will hold the hawk on his fist until such time as the falconer calls the hawk to his glove, and the food placed thereon.

When the young hawk responds instantly to being called off its block, it is almost ready for flying free, i.e. without the creance. However, rather than simply letting the hawk fly at this stage, we add another link to the hawk's learning chain, and one which will provide a bit of an insurance policy against it deciding to explore over the horizon – we train it to the lure.

THE LURE

For longwings, a swung lure should be used, while for shortwings (except the diminutive sparrowhawk, which is far too small to take on a rabbit) and broadwings, we use a 'dummy bunny' at first, although later we also use a swung lure for these hawks. Even if it is not envisaged that a hawk should be flown at feathered quarry, the use of a swung lure is still extremely helpful, as it can be used to recall a hawk from a considerable distance, from where the hawk would not be able to see, and therefore respond to, a dummy bunny lure. For that reason, we train all our shortwings and broadwings to both the dummy bunny and the swung lure.

To introduce the hawk to the lure is simple and should be attempted once the hawk is responding well to the sessions of flying to the fist (while still on the creance). After a few flights to the fist, the hawk should be replaced on its block, with creance still attached, and a well garnished lure should be dropped about a metre in front of it. Normally, the hawk will jump straight onto the lure as soon as it sees the meat attached to the lure. If it does not, it will still have its eyes glued to the lure, and the falconer can make the lure irresistible to the hawk by simply 'twitching' the lure by pulling at the lure line, which he will have held securely and firmly in his hand. The hawk, while wanting the food, will be rather nervous at this new delivery method and will probably drop on the floor at the side of the lure, rather than directly onto the lure. If the falconer is lucky, the hawk may strike at the lure and bind to it with one foot. Normally, the hawk will not touch the lure, but crane its neck to try to take the meat attached to the lure. At this stage, the falconer must again tweak the lure line, gently, and this will make the hawk strike and 'foot' the lure. Sometimes, the hawk will hold the lure with both feet, but one is the norm at this stage. As the hawk bends to eat the food, the falconer must 'make in', i.e. carefully, slowly and keeping low, move towards the lure. As he does so, the falconer should keep the lure line taut, while holding a pick-up piece in his gloved hand. As the hawk finishes its food, the falconer must make ready to have it on his glove.

With a broadwing, this is best achieved by the falconer throwing a small pick-up piece on the floor in front of the hawk, just far enough away to ensure that it cannot get the food without leaving the lure. Once the hawk has stepped off the lure, the falconer should quickly, but without fuss, remove the lure, placing it in his bag or vest pocket. The falconer should then use another pick-up piece to get the hawk to jump on to his glove.

With a shortwing or a longwing, the falconer should use his foot to secure the lure to the ground, and then get the hawk to jump off the lure, and onto his garnished glove, where it will eat the pick-up piece.

The following day, after the successful introduction of a hawk to the lure, the falconer should reinforce the lesson. This can be done by the falconer affixing a piece of food to the lure and, during the training session, drop the garnished lure in clear sight of the hawk, but a little further away than previously. As, by now, the hawk will be able to make the connection between the lure and feed, it should fly directly at the lure. If it does this well, the falconer can then move up a step and either increase the distance or even drop the lure and then keep it moving slowly while the hawk flies at it. For a longwing, the lure can be slowly swung and then dropped onto the floor for the hawk to take.

Whenever we use the lure – swung or dummy bunny – and want the hawk to notice it and take it (and this will also apply later when the broadwing or shortwing is used to catch a flushed rabbit or hare), we always shout 'Ho!', and this should be incorporated into the hawk's training. Some falconers use whistles for this, but whichever the reader feels best suits, a suitable cue should be introduced at a fairly early point in the hawk's training.

On the lead up to the hawk's first free flight, the lure should be used once or twice in each training period, so that the hawk becomes familiar with but not bored by the lure, which will be used throughout the hawk's lifetime for further training, fitness work and so on.

When a broadwing or shortwing is free flying, it will need to be able to land in trees and on other tall perches, and a wise falconer will give his hawk the opportunity to try this *before* the hawk is flown free, i.e. while the hawk is still on the creance. While it is possible to do this by casting the hawk into a tree, the risk of the creance becoming entangled in the branches is high. This can have catastrophic consequences should the hawk become entwined in the creance or the creance become wrapped around a branch, effectively trapping the hawk in the tree until such time as the falconer can climb the tree and free his hawk – by this time, the hawk may well have become seriously injured. At The National Falconry School, we use a high perch (about three metres/ten feet) made from an old telegraph pole, for the early training of our hawks. As this perch has smooth sides and nothing on which the creance can become entangled, it is a far safer alternative than a tree. We cast the hawk onto the top of the high perch, and then call it off in the same manner as when it has been on other lower perches, at a distance of about six metres/twenty feet.

Providing that the broadwing or shortwing hawk has behaved to this point, this last exercise should not prove too difficult and most hawks will respond just as quickly from a high perch as they would from a lower one. However, should the hawk prove to be reluctant to make the flight, the falconer will need to spend a little more time on the earlier exercises (i.e. calling off from a low perch) and may even need to drop the hawk's weight a little. Once the hawk will respond instantly and fly to the falconer's fist from a high perch, the exercise should be repeated, this time using the lure. Again, all things being equal, the hawk will react in the same manner as it has from lower perches. If it does not, but hesitates, then the falconer should revert to using the lure with the hawk on a low perch and, again, the hawk's weight may need to be lowered slightly.

At this stage in their training, we affix a transmitter to our hawks, simply to get them accustomed to carrying one. We also fit permanent jesses to the hawk's aylmeri as a matter of course, in addition to the mews jesses it will wear, and which are used, in conjunction with the swivel, to tether the hawk.

FLYING FREE

When the hawk will respond well to the falconer's call from both low and high perches, and also react well to the lure from both types of perch, it is time for the hawk's first free flight. We always give the novice hawk slightly lower rations on the day before its first flight, as an added insurance measure.

On the big day, the hawk should be taken up, weighed and generally treated as it has been on other, less auspicious days; this includes the fitting of a working transmitter, fitted with new batteries. The hawk should then be taken to the flying area, where it will have the creance fastened to its jesses (incidentally, we never fasten the creance to the swivel, since this causes unnecessary tangles of the creance, as it becomes wrapped around the swivel when the hawk flies) and then the hawk will be called off the perch, to the falconer's fist. We do this twice with the creance in place. When the hawk lands on the falconer's glove for the second calling off, and while the hawk is feeding on the fist, we remove the mews jesses and the creance without making any fuss and without drawing the hawk's attention to the matter – as far as the hawk is concerned, it is still on the creance. We then carry it to the perch, walk away as normal, and call it to the glove.

This exercise should, provided the falconer has adhered to the proper training regime and ensured that each link in the hawk's learning chain is properly constructed before moving on the next, go in a text book manner and, once the hawk has been flown free from a low perch to the falconer's glove, it is time to move on to the next step – the high perch.

The free hawk is cast onto the high perch, and then the falconer moves off (about six metres/twenty feet) and calls the hawk to his garnished fist. Again, all should go according to plan and this exercise should be repeated two or three times. The hawk should then be cast onto the high perch, and the lure dropped in plain sight of the hawk, which should fly directly to the lure, 'killing' it, and then feeding on the attached piece of meat.

With longwings, we call off the tethered (i.e. with a creance attached) hawk from the low perch, remove the mews jesses, etc. then call the hawk off to the swung lure, which is swung and dropped onto the ground slightly to the left of the hawk's flight line, at the same time shouting 'Ho!' as the lure hits the ground. Once the hawk has caught the lure and fed, it is jumped to the glove for a small piece of food, and the exercise is repeated but, this time, the lure is swung and flung at the hawk's feet as it comes towards the falconer – most longwing hawks manage to catch the lure on their first attempt.

All these free-flying exercises should be carried out on a fairly calm day, and with the hawk flying into the breeze, to aid flight and give it more confidence.

For many novices, the first few free flights with a hawk are the most worrying, as the tyro believes that his hawk may now decide to fly away. While this is possible, it is highly unlikely, as the hawk has never been able to fly away before and, if it had attempted to, would have been stopped by the creance to which it was attached. When the creance is removed, the hawk does not know that it now has 100% liberty, and will act as though it is still on the creance, i.e. will not make any attempt to fly away. However, once the hawk has been flying free for a week or more, it becomes more confident, as too does the novice falconer, who finds himself lulled into a false sense of security, and this is the time when a young hawk can be lost. It is important to stay focused on the hawk's training, not to cut corners and not to take liberties. I have spoken with many novice falconers who, having had success in the early days of training the young hawk, have then decided that they need not give quite so much consideration to the hawk's flying weight. The consequence of such over-confidence can be either a lost hawk, too high in condition to want to return, or the death of a hawk which has been kept in too low condition. Neither of these scenarios should be acceptable to any falconer.

FOLLOWING ON

Once a broadwing or shortwing has mastered the foregoing exercises, it is ready for the next phase of training – following on.

For this exercise, we utilise fence posts around the School's grounds, although some falconers will use trees and others, drystone walling. We start with the hawk, by now happily flying free, but not yet fit, sitting on a fence post where we have placed a small piece of food. The falconer then walks down the fence into the wind, and places another small piece of food on the next fence post. At this point, the falconer will call the hawk and it will fly towards him, see the food and land on that fence post. The falconer then walks away again and, when he is about five metres (sixteen feet) away from the hawk and between fence posts, calls the hawk, which will fly towards him looking for food on the fence post. As it will not see any food, it will fly past the falconer, landing on the next fence post. This exercise is repeated, with food being given in an unpredictable manner, so that the hawk will not see any pattern developing and believe that at any time, it may be given more food. In this way, the hawk will learn to follow the falconer, who can stop calling it after just a short time, as it will soon learn to fly along the fence without too much encouragement. Once this exercise is learned, we do the same thing within a small wooded copse, calling the hawk from one tree but not always feeding it on the glove, and so it will fly ahead to the next tree.

Once the hawk has learned this exercise well, it can be taken for a cross-country walk, in much the same manner as a dog and, by so doing, its fitness and confidence will grow quickly.

If a hawk will not leave the initial perch without seeing the falconer proffering feed, the hawk will require a further small reduction in weight.

Longwings, on the other hand, should be encouraged to fly directly to the swung lure and catch it for no more than two or three flights, after which, as the hawk approaches the falconer swinging the lure, the lure should be snatched away. The hawk will fly past, wondering what has happened to the lure, and craning its neck to see where the lure is. As it does so, the falconer should serve the lure and shout 'Ho!', allowing the hawk to turn around and catch the lure. On the next occasion, the hawk can be allowed to fly a couple of circuits around the falconer before being given the lure; the next step is to snatch away the lure on several occasions on the same flight, gradually building up the hawk's fitness and confidence. To prevent boredom setting in with the hawk, it should not be given more than three or four such flights in any one session.

WORKING WITH DOGS

An English springer spaniel marking an occupied rabbit warren. The use of such dogs is highly recommended, and can increase the bag immensely.

As most falconers will use a dog in conjunction with their hawk, be it a shortwing, a broadwing or a longwing, it is essential that both hawk and dog are accustomed to each other at an early stage. We place a mature dog in a dog crate (cage) in full view of the novice hawk, at a very early stage and the hawk quickly learns to accept it. Once this happens, we walk close to the hawk with a dog securely on a collar and lead, gradually getting closer to the hawk. Next we have a falconer holding the hawk on his fist, with the hawk feeding, and the hawk is carried closer to the dog in stages, until it can be directly next to or above the dog without showing any apprehension whatsoever.

We carry out exactly the same training routine with each puppy we train for use with our hawks.

By habituating dogs and hawks so young, we believe that both accept each other more quickly and easily than waiting until one or other is grown up, having never experienced the other animal.

It is highly recommended that any reader wishing to learn more about the training of dogs for falconry purposes avails himself of one of the many specialist books on the subject, since space within this volume does not allow full details of this aspect of falconry to be adequately covered.

FERRETS

With shortwings and broadwings, particularly the Harris' hawk, the use of a ferret is essential to provide good sport, and hawks should be habituated to ferrets in much the same way as to a dog. Although I have heard many falconers claim that their hawks are 100% steady to ferrets, this statement should be taken with a large pinch of salt, and wise falconers will ensure that, when working hawks and ferrets together, one person is charged with the welfare of the ferrets and does not fly a hawk at the same time.

CHAPTER 5

FERRETS

TYPES

Properly cared for, ferrets can live for up to fourteen years, with an average working life of six to eight years. Although some falconers will have set ideas about which colour ferret is best for falconry purposes, to me, the colour of a ferret is immaterial. I want a ferret with the right characteristics for its job and for ease of handling. Having kept most varieties/colours of ferret, the one thing I know is that the colour of an animal's coat does not give any guarantees about the way the animal behaves. Almost without exception, when a ferret does not behave properly, it is as a direct result of its human handler. I would advise the reader to simply choose the ferret which most appeals.

Falconers will give conflicting views on what makes a good ferret. Some will tell you that white ferrets should never be used with hawks as they closely resemble the colour of day-old chicks, and this can lead to the hawks attacking the ferrets by mistake. They may also state that all albinos are susceptible to illnesses and generally weak, and so should be avoided at all costs.

Others will say that a fitchet (a ferret resembling the natural colour of its wild cousin, the polecat) is too wild and will never be handleable and, as the colouration of such a ferret is so similar to that of a wild rabbit, the hawk can easily get confused and attack the ferret.

You may also hear the often quoted (but false) view that only white ferrets should be worked, as their dark-coloured relatives cannot be easily seen when out working in dense cover. Equally, others will tell you the opposite: that, as most ferreting takes place in the winter months, only dark ferrets should be used, as white ferrets will not show up in the snow.

I like to see some variety in my ferret stock and, provided that the ferret is a good worker, I consider colour to be immaterial.

OBTAINING FERRETS

Jills (i.e. female ferrets) come into season in early spring, when the days begin to get longer and the nights shorter. Because of this, and despite the fact that some breeders alter the ferrets' photoperiod (ratio of day [light] to night [dark]) thereby enabling the animals to breed all year-round, young ferrets are normally only available at certain times of the year, i.e. during the summer months. This is the best time to buy young ferrets, properly known as kits.

You may see ferrets advertised for sale at other times of the year but, unless they are bred by someone who has tweaked the animal's photoperiod, they will obviously not be kits, and, all too often, the reason for the ferrets appearing on the market is because they have proved less than suitable for their current owners. I would advise the reader to leave these animals alone, although I am aware that some – a very small minority in my experience – are being sold for bona fide reasons, and will make good purchases. I recommend that the reader should buy kits of between eight to twelve weeks.

Ferrets are sold by many people, from the person who lovingly cares for his animals

The author digging out a ferret. Without a ferret finder, it would be impossible to know when and where to dig for a missing ferret. This one had killed a rabbit underground, but was also holding another (live) rabbit behind the dead coney.

and simply breeds one or two litters a year to ensure continuation of his line, to commercial breeders who have many hundreds of ferrets kept and bred in order to make money for their owners. In between these two extremes are many others, who include good and bad ferret-keepers, all with their own reasons for breeding and selling the animals.

It is sound advice that, wherever possible, one should go to an established ferret breeder who has a proven reputation, and who has been keeping and breeding ferrets for several years. While no such person will let you have their very best ferrets – they will want to keep those for their own purposes – neither will they risk a hard-earned reputation by selling you inferior stock.

When buying ferrets, try to visit the breeder's establishment, and look carefully at the parents of the kits being offered for sale, along with any other ferrets kept by the seller. All cages should be clean, of an adequate size and not overcrowded. Look at the latrine corner: the faeces should be hard, dark brown, and have only a slight smell. Examine all of the adults; are they tame? If not, then the breeder has probably not handled them enough, and may simply be keeping them for breeding to make money. If the adults are not handleable, it is highly likely the kits will be the same.

Are they all in good condition? What are they being fed on? Many people feed their ferrets on totally unsuitable diets and malnourished animals do not make good workers.

A healthy ferret will have energy and a *joie de vivre*, bouncing around its cage and playing with its siblings. Its eyes will be bright, ears held erect, coat shiny and clean, while an ill ferret will be entirely the opposite – lethargic and lying down asleep for most of the day. An ill ferret's ears will be flat against its head, its coat matted, dirty and greasy to the touch; it may have a discharge from its eyes, ears, sex opening or anus, and it may also have diarrhoea.

Do not buy any such ferrets nor any of its cage mates.

How many ferrets are needed by a falconer to enable him to pursue his hobby? I believe that the optimum number of ferrets to start with is a trio – i.e. one hob (male) and two jills (females). Unless the falconer wishes to breed his ferrets, the hob should be vasectomised, allowing him to mate the jills, thus taking them out of season without producing unwanted kits (see page 80-1 for more details).

Hobs and jills work differently from each other: jills tend to be quick, often leaving a few rabbits in the warren, while hobs tend to be slower, often not fast enough to flush all the rabbits. By working both sexes together, one has the advantage of both characteristics and they complement each other.

SEXING FERRETS

The sexing of ferrets is simplicity itself, even in very young animals. In the jill, the vaginal opening and the anus are very close together, whereas in the hob, the penal opening and the anus are far apart. In addition, the hob is bigger and stockier, with a very broad head, while the smaller jill has a slight build with a slender head.

Size is another potentially contentious area, with some people favouring large ferrets while others go for much smaller types. I believe that ferrets can be either too big or too small, and recommend that this is taken into consideration when making one's choice of kits. Remember that the kits' parents will be a guide to the size of their offspring.

From an early age, ferret kits must be handled gently but carefully. With this type of treatment they will soon learn that your hands are wonderful, but not for biting. The kits will come to trust you and look forward to your handling them. Throughout the time spent handling the kits, one should speak in a soft and soothing tone of voice, while at the same time stroking them. I also get them used to being picked up, particularly with the hand coming straight for the ferret's head, as this is what will happen to them once they begin their rabbiting careers.

When picking up a ferret, place one hand around its torso, with the thumb and first finger around the neck and the other hand under its backside, to take the animal's weight. To help soothe and relax the ferret, gently swing it with the hand under its arms gently stroking its body by pulling it through the other hand which was under its backside. This method works with even the most uncooperative of ferrets, even adults. With tamer ones, a few minutes of this treatment will induce a soporific state, rather like the 'dizzying' of a chicken or pigeon.

At first, ferrets unused to being handled may struggle and try to escape. At such times, do not increase the pressure on the ferret's body to try to prevent it from moving, as this may well cause injury to the ferret, which will also be extremely tempted to bite the hand administering this treatment.

HOUSING

Ferrets living out of doors must be supplied with a fully weatherproof cage, which is big enough, and of the correct dimensions, to allow the ferrets to indulge in their natural behaviour, and it should be remembered that ferrets are three-dimensional animals, and like to climb.

There are two main types of housing for ferrets: one is the 'ferret cub' (a hutch), and the other the 'ferret court' (an aviary-type cage). Our ferrets live in ferret courts throughout the winter, but in the summer (i.e. breeding season), the hobs are housed in separate cubs, i.e. one hob to a cage.

Ferret Cubs

These are simply well-built hutches, similar to the type in which pet rabbits are kept. The minimum size for a cub suitable for three ferrets (as described earlier) is 1.5 x 0.75 x 0.75 m (5 x 2½ x 2½ ft), although larger cubs can be advantageous to both ferrets and their human owners. Some keepers supply a nest box, but this is not essential. If a nest box is supplied, it can be fixed to the outside of the cub, thus giving more space for the ferrets to live, or it may form an integral part of the cub. Access to the nest box should be through a small 'pop-hole', measuring about 10 cm (4 inches) in diameter.

The doors to the cubs are made from a wooden frame covered with strong welded wire mesh, of about 1 cm (½ inch) square.

Ferret courts

These are like aviaries, and ours measure 3 x 2 x 2 m (9¾ x 6½ x 6½ ft) wide, thus giving the ferrets plenty of space to exercise. We use a concrete floor which prevents the ferrets from scraping their way out of the cage, while also allowing adequate cleaning, and thus prevents the build-up of potentially harmful bacteria. We always supply at least one nest box in each court, and plenty of tubes, branches and old tree roots. We consider this to be a kind of adventure playground where the ferrets can exercise and practise their hunting skills.

The wire used for the courts is the same as that used on our cubs, i.e. strong welded mesh of about 1 cm (½ inch) squares.

FEEDING

Ferrets can be fed on a diet consisting of either complete carcasses, e.g. rabbits, pigeons, etc., or one of the many available complete diet pellets.

Our ferrets are – and have been since 1994 – fed solely on a complete diet pelleted ferret feed. We use James Wellbeloved *'Ferret Complete'*, and have found that this well-designed and well-produced ferret feed is perfect for our ferrets, whatever the age or use of the ferrets, from young kits to OAPs and working adult ferrets.

A great advantage we have found of using pelleted food is that our ferrets will not eat other food, e.g. rabbits. This is due to the fact that ferrets exhibit olfactory imprinting, and will only eat the feed they are used to. In practical terms, this means that, should a pellet-fed ferret kill a rabbit while working underground, it will not stop to eat the rabbit, but simply leave it and continue to ferret through the warren. This reduces the necessity to dig out a 'laid up' ferret.

WATER

Essential for the well-being of the ferrets, we always ensure that the animals have access to a constant supply of clean, fresh drinking water. In the courts, we use poultry appliances for this, while in the cubs we supply water via gravity-feed drinking bottles, securely fixed on the outside of the wire netting doors of the cubs.

TRAINING

By supplying our ferrets with pipes, tubes and old tree roots in their courts, we believe that they are being trained for rabbiting purposes all the time they are moving around or playing in the courts. When the kits are first placed in the courts, we occasionally

An adult ferret (front) with a young kit; this is the ideal way to introduce young ferrets to working, as they will follow the experienced ferret and thus learn their job.

put some food into the pipes, etc., and hide some under the tree roots. The ferrets soon find these titbits, and eagerly search for more.

When we first take a ferret on rabbiting operations, we use an experienced ferret with a younger inexperienced one. The youngster simply follows and imitates his senior, and soon picks up the game. Early outings for ferrets are always in small rabbit warrens, so as not to overface the young tyro.

JILLS AND OESTRUS

In common with many other animals – including chickens and horses – the ferret's oestrus is regulated by photoperiodism. In other words, she will 'come on heat' when the days get longer, and the nights shorter, i.e. in the spring. Unless taken out of season – either by injection of hormones or by mating – she will remain in season throughout the summer months.

If a jill is not mated immediately she is on heat, the levels of oestrogen (the female sex hormone) will build up, causing progressive depression of the bone marrow. This can result in a condition known as *pancytopaenia* – the abnormal depression of all three cell types of the blood – a condition that is potentially fatal. In other words, if a jill is left in oestrus ('on heat') for any length of time, she will almost inevitably die before reaching her full life expectancy.

Where the owner of the jill does not wish to have a litter from his ferrets, the animals are best neutered (both jills and hobs). Neutering will also reduce the smell of the animals (particularly during the summer months), reduce the risk of fighting between hobs, and allow any combination of ferrets to be kept together in relative safety.

However, if it is desirable to keep open all options, the best methods of removing the risk of serious health problems linked to prolonged oestrogenic exposure are to either have the jill mated with a vasectomised male ferret (a hoblet), or given a 'jill-jab' (a hormone injection) by a vet.

To have a hob vasectomised can be relatively expensive, but a hoblet will be able to take jills out of oestrus for between seven and eight years, thereby repaying this investment several times over. Savings will also be made on the food, time and trouble that the kits would cause the owner and, of course, there will be fewer unwanted ferrets to be abandoned by unscrupulous people.

A jill mated with a hoblet will usually have a pseudo-pregnancy (phantom or false pregnancy) following the mating. This may result in the jill's stomach swelling, she may produce milk and she may nest-build. In other words, she may exhibit all of the symptoms of being pregnant, with one major difference – at the end of the 42-day 'pregnancy', she will not produce a litter. The jill will, however, come back into oestrus about three to four weeks after the end of the pseudo-pregnancy, when she will require mating again. By the end of the second 'pregnancy', the summer will be almost over, and the jill will not come on heat again until the following spring.

The reason that a hoblet can take the jill out of season, without getting her pregnant, is that ferrets are induced ovulators, i.e. the physical act of mating induces the jill to ovulate. As the hoblet cannot produce sperm to fertilise the eggs, the jill comes out of season without becoming pregnant.

Some ferret clubs recommend and even encourage owners of hoblets to lend them to owners of jills on heat, but this practice is fraught with dangers. The risk of the spread of diseases such as Aleutian disease, distemper, enteritis and influenza is far too great. Encouraging the loan of hoblets simply dissuades people from making the investment for themselves, and is not a sign of responsible animal ownership.

If owners do not wish to invest in a hoblet of their own, or have only a small number of jills, 'jill jabs' – injections with drugs such as proligestone (Delvosteron®) – are often a viable alternative which allows owners to keep their options open, without endangering their ferrets or producing unwanted litters. One of the few side-effects of hormone injections is temporary hair loss at the injection site. Sometimes jills will need more than one such injection during a year, i.e. if they come back into season.

Some ferret-keepers have other ideas for taking their jills out of season – some of which are extremely outlandish. One theory is that, if a suitably shaped stone or similar object is placed in the cage with a jill who is on heat, she will copulate with it, bringing herself out of season, and thus reducing any health risks. Others state that if two or more jills are kept together, and never allowed the company of a male ferret, they will 'turn lesbian' and remove each other from heat by using their paws on each other. Some ferret owners even try to simulate the coitus of a hob by gripping the jill firmly by the neck and using either a glass rod or even a cotton bud to stimulate the vagina; there is obviously a great risk of injury to the jill – and very little hope of success – in such actions, which should not be attempted by anyone.

Of course, no credence should be given to any of these weird theories, but it is easy to understand why the users of such methods believe they work.

Although a jill comes into season early in the spring, and will remain so until she is removed from season by a mating or hormone injection, the obvious signs of her condition will not always be present. When she first comes into season, her vulva will swell noticeably, often protruding from her body by over a centimetre (half an inch). Within seven to ten days of mating, this swelling will reduce, but it will also reduce (albeit temporarily) after a couple of weeks even if she is not mated. This does not, however, mean that she is not in season as, in the next few weeks, her vulva will again swell to very large proportions.

WORKING TACTICS

On the morning of rabbiting operations, the ferrets should be fed as normal – we also feed the ferrets when we stop for our lunch, to prevent them from getting too tired and hungry to be able to carry out their work. We always appoint one person to be in charge of the ferrets, to ensure their well-being during the day. While this person may be changed at some time in the day, there is always one such person with sole and total responsibility for the ferrets and ferreting.

A jill ferret in a carry box. It is important to give some comfort and safety to all ferrets taken on hunting forays, and only boxes do this.

We transport our ferrets in well-ventilated wooden carry boxes, lined with a handful of fresh straw and, if the weather is particularly cold, we give extra straw.

Once we are in the vicinity of the rabbit warren we are to work, we will keep extremely quiet and look for signs of recent rabbit activity. Well-used warrens will have no webs over the openings, nor any build-up of dead leaves in the mouths of the tunnels; there will also be a plentiful supply of fresh rabbit droppings. Once we are sure that there is evidence of recent rabbit activity, we quietly loft the hawks, and then place a minimum of two ferrets (both equipped with ferret detector collars) in the workings, with one at each extremity of the workings.

When a rabbit bolts, we shout 'Ho!' to signal to the hawk that a rabbit is out, although this is usually totally unnecessary, as the hawks see far better than we do and are often giving chase as we shout. When a hawk catches a rabbit, it is important that the falconer be close enough to kill the rabbit (if the hawk has not already done so) as quickly and humanely as possible, and before the hawk can be injured by the thrashing rabbit.

Equipment

An albino jill (female) ferret, equipped with a Deben Ferret Finder III, prior to being used for bolting rabbits for hawks.

Do not be tempted to carry too much equipment, but neither should you leave behind equipment which you may need. Below are details of the essential equipment necessary for a successful day's ferreting:

• Ferret carry box – strong but light, and with good ventilation. A good carry box will help ensure that the ferrets are comfortable and safe between their trips underground. The box should be lined with straw, and a water bottle can be affixed to the outside of the box when the ferrets are resting.

• Ferret detector – essential wear for every ferret: without this collar, how will you know where the missing ferret is, and whether you will need to dig it out? Ensure that the batteries are working well, with enough power to last should the ferret stay underground at the end of the day, necessitating a return trip by the ferreter on the next day.

• Graft or spade – we use ex-Army spades with short handles, dished and pointed blades, and a T-piece at the end of the handle. Grinding an edge on the blade will help chop though the inevitable tree roots. To ensure that you don't lose the graft, paint the handle in a bright or fluorescent paint.

• Knife – essential for killing captured rabbits and for gutting and skinning the cadavers.

• Ferret food and water – when you stop for your lunch, give the ferrets theirs, and they will have enough energy to work through the day, thus giving you great sport.

• Torch – if the ferret lays up, then a torch may be necessary to help in its recovery.

• First aid kit – for both humans and animals (i.e. ferrets, dogs and hawks). At least one member of the team should also have the expertise to use the equipment in the kit.

• Live catch trap – a live catch trap is extremely useful for capturing ferrets which have been lost while on rabbiting forays.

CHAPTER 6
EQUIPMENT

As with all new endeavours, a certain amount of equipment is essential. This chapter lists the main items required by a falconer, although the list is by no means definitive, as individuals will have their own needs, requirements and ideas, and a falconer will be constantly looking to improve his kit list in an effort to improve his falconry activities.

SCALES

As detailed throughout this book, one of the most important aspects of flying a raptor is the weight of the bird. Indeed, many modern falconry books advise that a set of accurate scales is *the* most important item of equipment (a sentiment with which I am in full agreement). This has not always been so, however, and authors such as Gilbert Blaine (*Falconry*, 1936) mention scales almost as an aside. In his book, Blaine states 'A useful guide is to weigh a hawk on a scales.' Thankfully, by the time we get to M. H. Woodford (*A Manual of Falconry*, 1960), ideas seem to have changed somewhat, and he states, 'Weighing Machine – This is one of the most important pieces of equipment.'

It must, however, be mentioned that weighing alone will not be sufficient to ensure that any hawk is in flying condition. To do this, one must also judge the hawk's condition by feeling its muscles, and watching its behaviour. I am always amazed, frightened and appalled when I read books which purport to give specific flying weights for hawks. Every hawk is an individual, and the correct flying weight for one is not necessarily the correct weight for another, even if it is of the same species and gender. For instance, I fly a cast of male Harris' hawks (*Parabuteo unicinctus*), which coincidentally are siblings from the same clutch. One flies at 125 g (5 oz) higher than its brother. While it could be argued that one hawk is smaller than 'normal' and the other is larger than 'normal', this merely begs the question – what is the 'normal' weight? The answer, of course, is that there is no such figure.

Today, there is a plethora of scales designed for falconry use, although some are obviously better suited than others. Some falconers, including myself, favour the 'traditional' balance scales, while others, wanting a higher degree of accuracy, believe that one of the modern digital scales will give a more accurate weight. Some falconers will claim that they need to weigh their hawks to the utmost degree of accuracy, and insist that the weight of a hawk should be so precise that it should be weighed to 0.1 g. While this is laudable, it is also completely impractical and naïve in the extreme to believe that this can be done. What happens if a hawk mutes just as the bird is being placed on the scales? This will reduce its weight by several grams. What if the hawk had muted immediately after weighing? Which weight should then be taken as the 'true' weight? I'm sure you see my point.

I also know of several falconers who use spring balance scales. This, to me, is nonsensical as springs can, and do, stretch, and the accuracy of these scales will undoubtedly be compromised by wear. If spring scales are used, they will need to be calibrated at least every three months, and even then will require the springs replacing every couple of years, and still not give truly accurate readings consistently.

Before looking at the various types of scales available, and at the pros and cons, it is prudent to remind the reader that a falconer should weigh his hawks every twenty-four hours. It is important that the weighing is carried out at a consistent time, and in a consistent manner, to ensure that the hawk's guts are empty of food, and that any casting has been regurgitated.

TRADITIONAL BALANCE SCALES

I am always cautious about using the term 'traditional', as it is used far too often in a completely misleading sense. Although many falconers will describe the counter-balance type scales, with a platform for weights on one side and a perch on the other, as traditional, I can find no date at which falconers began using any scales, or weighing the hawks at all. In *Falconry in the British Isles* (1855), F. H. Salvin and W. Brodrick do not mention scales, weighing or weight of hawks, referring only to the condition of yarak and describing how this can be identified in various species. I always smile when a falconer accuses me and my staff of thumbing our noses at tradition by using the metric system of weighing our hawks, i.e. we weigh in grams. If, as I suspect, weighing of hawks only originated less than one hundred years ago, no weighing can be accurately described as 'traditional'. For reference, the Oxford English Dictionary (OED) defines tradition as *'an opinion or belief or custom handed down … from ancestors to posterity, especially orally or by practice'*. Not very enlightening.

Counter-balance scales are, I believe, the most common and popular type of scales among falconers, particularly those of middle age or older. My first pair was made from an old set that my mother no longer has a use for, as she had been bought a set of 'new fangled' scales and thought that the old set were now obsolete. My mother had inherited the old set from her mother, and kept them simply for sentimental reasons, as a kind of decoration on one of the shelves in the kitchen. The scales were extremely big and bulky, and the weights were made from solid brass. I am sure the accuracy of the scales and the weights was somewhat questionable, but as a boy of eleven years, I probably overlooked the shortcomings of the scales, happy that my mother had allowed me to make use of them. Mother was not, however, too happy when she realised that I needed to alter them to accommodate the weighing of my kestrel.

With the help of my father, I removed the pan from one side of the scales and replaced it with a wooden perch, padded with leather. After making this modification, I needed to alter the balancing part (the scales had a large screw underneath which accomplished this), and I was ready to go.

I loved the scales – they looked extremely impressive and I got many looks of envy from friends who didn't have hawks, but still admired my scales. The simple life of a young boy in the mid-1960s bears little resemblance to that of a twenty-first century child. At some time in the 1970s, while I was serving in the forces, the scales were lost and I consequently had to buy a new set.

The beauty of counter-balance scales is that, provided one has accurate weights, the scales are almost completely foolproof and will last indefinitely. When buying a set, choose one that has been properly made, and not one cobbled together from kitchen scales. Also, get one with a large footprint, and that is heavy and strong enough to weigh any hawk. While a large set of scales will work for a small hawk, a small set will be useless when, for example, weighing an eagle or even a large longwing.

SPRING BALANCE SCALES

As stated earlier, these scales have no place with a falconer. Springs stretch over time, and the accuracy of spring scales will even vary with temperatures. And don't just take my word for it. In his book *Understanding the Bird of Prey* (a must-have for any serious falconer), Dr Nick Fox states 'spring balances are untrustworthy'.

DIGITAL SCALES

If you are the kind of person who believes that everything modern is better than anything else, particularly if the item is more than two years old, you will probably use (or at least *try* to use) a set of digital scales.

Here at The National Falconry School, we use digital scales for only one falconry purpose: we weigh all our eggs, and the newly hatched eyasses, on digital scales. The accuracy of such scales is essential for such purposes. However, once the youngsters get to a stage where they move a lot, we have great difficulty in getting an accurate reading, as every movement of the hawk causes the scales to vary tremendously. We have tried a very expensive set, which had a 'damper' to reduce this problem, but even these we found impossible to use on anything other than very young eyasses.

There are some very good digital scales on the market that are suitable for falconers to use in weighing their birds, but I have yet to find any good enough – and easy enough – to use to get consistently accurate readings from our range of hawks.

SELECTING THE SCALES FOR YOU

Whichever type of scales you decide upon, when selecting scales for falconry use, try to judge your needs for the foreseeable future, and not simply your present requirements and hawks. Most falconers will fly several different species of hawk during their falconry career, and the scales should be able to accommodate any hawk, of just about any size and weight.

It is also worth chatting to other falconers and trying the scales that they favour, to see if they meet with your approval. Remember, though, that what suits one, may not suit another and also bear in mind the practical aspects of weighing hawks using the different types of scales available.

Don't penny-pinch; good scales will last a lifetime, and so they should be considered as an investment. Keep them clean, sparingly oiled and correctly stored, and they will repay your investment many times over. The weights for counter-balance scales must be looked after. Dropping such weights can result in pieces being broken off, and even small amounts of damage can render weights inaccurate over the years of usage. It is also worthwhile, about every twelve months or so, having all of the weights checked for accuracy, and many specialist retailers of scales will offer this service.

FREEZER

Another essential item for the falconer is a good, reliable freezer: some falconers favour chest freezers, while others favour upright models. It does not matter which type of freezer one chooses, as long as it is in good working order and totally reliable. Buying second-hand freezers may seem like a good cost-saving measure, but such practice is fraught with danger, as one has no way of knowing the exact age of the freezer and its condition. Obviously, as the freezer ages, it is more liable to mechanical failure. If it is full of hawk feed when it fails, any savings made in its purchase will be lost immediately. One will also then have to source more feed (and another freezer), while trying to ensure that the hawks are fed.

We run four freezers to cater for all our hawk-feeding requirements, and ensure that we use the feed in the order in which we purchase it, i.e. we use correct stock rotation methods. Our system also means that we have one freezer standing idle at any one time, in order to ensure that we can properly clean the freezers between deliveries of feed, and also as insurance – should one of four freezers fail, we have enough spare space to relocate the frozen food to the spare freezer. We also use electronic sensors and warning devices to alert us to any mains failure or the unacceptable rise in temperature of any freezers, i.e. when the freezer fails.

Although many novice falconers will believe that they can get by simply by utilising part of the human family's domestic freezer, this is not acceptable. Who would really want to eat a steak from a freezer where it has been stored next to rats, mice, etc?

The freezer does not have to be large, simply big enough to store enough feed for one's hawk(s) to last about four to six weeks, and there are many suitable models of freezer available.

JESSES AND ANKLETS/AYLMERI

Items fitted to a hawk are known as 'furniture', and jesses are included in this group. Jesses are the straps used for controlling the hawk, and come in a variety of styles and of different materials. It is highly recommended that, even though ready-made hawk furniture is available via a few clicks on a manufacturer's website, the true falconer learns and masters making these items. As there are many excellent books available which detail such practice (See Bibliography page 165), I do not intend to detail such methods within this volume.

The 'traditional' method of putting jesses on a hawk called for them to be fitted directly onto the hawk's legs (actually on their feet), but this has been mainly superseded by the use of aylmeri, often referred to simply as anklets. These were first invented and used by Major Guy Aylmer (hence the name) who came up with the idea while Conservator of Forests in Sudan. It is said that, while flying red-headed merlins (*Falco chicquera*), other birds, believing the trailing jesses to be snakes, attacked the merlins. He determined to find a method of retaining control over his hawks, while eliminating the need for long trailing jesses, and he came up with anklets, which are today named after the major, i.e. they are known as aylmeri.

Normally made from some sort of leather, usually but not always kangaroo skin, the size of the aylmeri is obviously determined by the size of the hawk and, while it is possible to purchase ready-made aylmeri, to ensure the best fit for any hawk, it is preferable to make them to measure. Once cut to size and shape, several small slits should be made along the central part of each aylmeri, both top and bottom. These slits will ensure that, as the hawk moves, the top and bottom edges of the aylmeri will curl over, giving a smooth edge which will not be harmful to the hawk. Were this not to be done, as the leather hardens through normal usage, the material would become extremely hard and the solid edges would create an almost knife-like edge which can seriously damage the legs of the hawk.

The aylmeri are held in place by brass eyelets and through these are fastened the jesses. The standard jesses used exclusively up to about ten to fifteen years ago were made of leather and consisted of two types – mews jesses and field jesses. Mews jesses have a button on one end, with a slit in the other end; this slit is used to attach the swivel, through which the leash is threaded. As mews jesses have a slit, it is possible for hawks flown with these slit jesses in place to become hooked up on branches and other similar objects, while they are being flown. For this reason, no one should ever fly hawks with mews jesses attached. I am amazed, however, how many falconers do fly their hawks with mews jesses. There are several falconry books, written by experienced falconers, which show photographs of hawks with mews jesses attached being flown. This is sheer stupidity, especially as the authors almost always make a point, within the same book, of stating that such actions are indefensible and show a total lack of professionalism on the part of the offending falconer. Mews jesses should be removed prior to flying a hawk and replaced by flying jesses, without a slit.

Some falconers attach permanent or field jesses to the hawk's aylmeri. These jesses are simply plain pieces of leather with neither buttons nor slits, and are left attached to the aylmeri at all times.

The latest idea in jesses is to use ones made from nylon, and which thread through the eyelets, with the other end attached to the swivel, which in turn is attached to the leash. With these nylon jesses, one may either use permanent jesses or flying jesses for when the hawk is to be flown.

The length of the jesses is extremely important: jesses that are too short prevent the tethered hawk from moving adequately, while over-long jesses can easily cause the hawk to straddle its block and become trapped. During struggles to free its legs, the hawk will inevitably damage its feathers. Large block and short jesses are the order of the day to ensure the well-being of the hawk.

I must mention so-called 'false aylmeri' and their use. False aylmeri are made in a similar way to normal aylmeri, but due to their construction, have two brass eyelets in each aylmeri, as opposed to one in each normal aylmeri. These eyelets are therefore heavy, and tend to hang lower on the hawk's foot, and as such create the perfect opportunity for the hawk to catch its back toe in the eyelets. This can – and usually does – have disastrous consequences. For this reason, I see no real use for false aylmeri. Hawks fitted with these cannot be left with them fitted while in mews or aviaries, if one is to safeguard the well-being of the hawk.

JESS GREASE AND LEATHER TREATMENTS

All leather, whether it be buckskin, kangaroo, calf or any other type of animal skin, will become brittle with use and age, particularly when it is allowed to get wet (e.g. when the hawk is bathing). Hardened leather will break easily, and may even damage the hawk (e.g. when aylmeri become hard and brittle). For this reason, it is essential that all furniture made from animal skin is treated regularly with a suitable leather treatment or conditioner. Such treatments are readily available from falconry furniture manufacturers and saddlery shops and outlets.

SWIVELS

The swivel links the leash and the jesses, and so is vitally important. As in anything, the weakest link will always fail, and so when one has fitted top-quality aylmeri, jesses and leash, it would be foolish to fit an inferior swivel – and yet many falconers do. I have seen falconers, presumably in an attempt to save money, use totally inadequate 'cheap' swivels. These useless pieces of metal range from swivels designed for dogs and cats, to those made for lures, to those made for fishing tackle – the only thing they have in common is that they are not fit for purpose.

Properly designed and made swivels may cost more than the rubbish described above, but are definitely worth the investment. Proper falconry swivels will last a long time, and are rarely known to fail. Such swivels are made from either brass or stainless steel, and I favour the latter.

Swivels come in different sizes for different hawks, and also in slightly different shapes. Some are rounded, others square while yet others are pointed. Try out each type and then settle on the type which you find best suits you and your falconry activities, but be sure they are made by a reputable falconry furniture manufacturer, for the safety and well-being of all concerned.

At least one spare swivel should be kept for

A standard leash threaded through the hawk's swivel.

each hawk, as these small but essential items of falconry equipment are all too easily lost. To help prevent this loss, when using traditional jesses which necessitate the removal of the swivel before the hawk can be flown, the falconer should thread the swivel onto the leash, which is then folded and tied to the falconer's belt, bag or waistcoat.

LEASH

While a leash is simply a short length of rope or cord, there are three main designs of leash used in modern falconry.

THE TRADITIONAL LEASH

In the past, these leashes were made from leather, but this material is not best suited for this purpose as, after some use, the leather tends to break without warning.

Modern leashes of the 'traditional' design are made from nylon cord or rope, and will last for many years, although they should be checked for wear and tear on a daily basis, and discarded and replaced if any wear or damage is found.

For young hawks, some falconers like to modify the design slightly, by sewing a piece of elastic across a bight (or loop) of the leash, and this elastic then acts as a shock absorber. Such a device is useful where a young hawk, its leg bones not yet fully formed and therefore not as strong as an adult's bones, bates strongly. However, most falconers will simply ensure that such a hawk is tethered on a short leash, which will ensure that the hawk cannot bate strongly enough to damage its legs.

Traditional leashes are tied with the falconer's knot, and it is essential that every falconer master the tying of this basic knot very early in their falconry career.

To tie the falconer's knot, which of necessity is tied with one hand, follow the details below, in conjunction with the set of photographs detailing the actions required.

For right-handed falconers

Tying the falconer's knot with the right hand.

Stage 1 – With the right hand, pass the end of the leash through the ring on the block or bow, from right to left, until the desired length of leash has been passed through. Then pass the end of the leash over the first finger of the right hand and down between the first and second finger.

Stage 2 – Put the right thumb over the leash where the leash passes through the bow/block ring, and then under the leash as it emerges at the other side of the ring.

Stage 3 – Raise the thumb to make a loop in the leash.

With the hawk sitting on the left (gloved fist), and its jesses between finger and thumb, move close to the intended perch. With the right hand, pass the end of the leash through the ring on the block or bow, from right to left, until the desired length of leash has been passed through. It is always best to tie a fairly short leash, with the hawk having enough length of leash to be able to jump on and off the bow or perch, and to reach its water, but the leash should not be long enough to allow the hawk to gain much momentum when it bates, as this may well lead to injured legs for the hawk, particularly a young hawk.

Pass the end of the leash over the first finger of the right hand, and down between the first and second finger. Put the right thumb over the leash where the leash passes through the bow/block ring, and then under the leash as it emerges at the other side of the ring. Raise the thumb to make a loop in the leash, and then, using the first two fingers of the right hand, take the end of the leash around the right of the bight of the leash (the loop formed by the leash as it passes through the ring) to the end of the thumb. Using the thumb, pull a small loop of the leash through the space occupied by the thumb, forming a small loop. Leaving the loop, pass the end of the leash through the loop to 'lock' the knot.

Stage 4 – Using the first two fingers of the right hand, take the end of the leash around the right of the bight of the leash (the loop formed by the leash as it passes through the ring) to the end of the thumb.

Stage 5 – Using the thumb, pull a small loop of the leash through the space occupied by the thumb, forming a small loop.

Stage 6 – Leaving the loop, pass the end of the leash through the loop to 'lock' the knot.

For left-handed falconers

With the hawk sitting on the right (gloved fist), and with its jesses between finger and thumb, move close to the intended perch. With the left hand, pass the end of the leash through the ring on the block or bow, from left to right, until the desired length of leash has been passed through. It is always best to tie a fairly short leash, with the

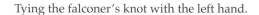

Tying the falconer's knot with the left hand.

Stage 1 – With the left hand, pass the end of the leash through the ring on the block or bow, from left to right, until the desired length of leash has been passed through.

Stage 2 – Pass the end of the leash over the first finger of the left hand, and down between the first and second finger and put the left thumb over the leash where the leash passes through the bow/block ring, and then under the leash as it emerges at the other side of the ring.

Stage 3 – Raise the thumb to make a loop in the leash, and then – Stage 4 – using the first two fingers of the left hand, take the end of the leash around the left of the bight of the leash (the loop formed by the leash as it passes through the ring) to the end of the thumb.

Stage 5 – Using the thumb, pull a small loop of the leash through the space occupied by the thumb…

…forming a small loop.

Stage 6 – Finally, leaving the loop, pass the end of the leash through the loop to 'lock' the knot.

hawk having enough length of leash to be able to jump on and off the bow or perch, and to reach its water, but the leash should not be long enough to allow the hawk to gain much momentum when it bates, as this may well lead to injured legs for the hawk, particularly a young hawk.

Pass the end of the leash over the first finger of the left hand, and down between the first and second finger. Put the left thumb over the leash where the leash passes through the bow/block ring, and then under the leash as it emerges at the other side of the ring. Raise the thumb to make a loop in the leash, and then, using the first two fingers of the left hand, take the end of the leash around the left of the bight of the leash (the loop formed by the leash as it passes through the ring) to the end of the thumb. Using the thumb, pull a small loop of the leash through the space occupied by the thumb, forming a small loop. Leaving the loop, pass the end of the leash through the loop to 'lock' the knot.

Some hawks become extremely adept at attacking and unfastening these knots, and it is advisable to tie two such knots in each leash, always ensuring that they are properly locked by threading the end of the leash through the final loop. To ensure a tidy job, and also provide a little more reassurance, we always tie the end of the leash onto itself via a simple loop knot.

THE LOOP LEASH

Based on an Arab design, the loop leash gets rid of the necessity for, and the uncertainty of, the falconer's knot. (However every falconer must be 100% proficient at tying the falconer's knot, which will have a myriad of uses throughout one's falconry career.) Also, the 'traditional' leash can easily become tangled, often leading to injury for the hawk, whereas the loop leash does not tangle so easily. However, the loop leash is not, to my mind, as

Fastening the button leash. Stage 1 – The leash is passed through the hawk's swivel.

Stage 2 –The end of the leash is passed through the ring on the bow perch.

Stage 3 – The end of the button leash is passed though the hawk's swivel again.

Stage 4 – The loop of the leash is passed over the button.

Stage 5 – The loop is pulled down onto the bow perch ring.

quick and easy to unfasten as the traditional leash, and so we never use loop leashes on very young hawks.

On one end of the loop leash is the loop, while on the other is a button; this button can be made from a large leather washer, a moulded plastic disc or a similar object. With the hawk sitting on the gloved fist, and its jesses held firmly under the thumb, the loop end is threaded through the hawk's swivel, through the bow/block ring and then doubled back on itself. The looped end is then passed through the swivel again, but this time in the opposite direction and the loop is passed over the button. By applying slight pressure, the loop is pulled back through the swivel and fastens around the bow/block ring.

HYBRID LEASHES

While both the 'traditional' and loop leash have their advantages, both also have their disadvantages, and a couple of falconry furniture manufacturers have hybridised the two in an attempt to get the best of both. The result is a leash with a loop at one end, and a simple point on the other. The manufacturers' rationale is that, where the leash has a button, it can become tangled fairly easily, but a loop will aid the fastening of the leash, and so the hybrid is their answer to this problem.

A hybrid leash is fitted by threading the end of the leash through the hawk's swivel and then through the leash's loop, thus fastening it to the swivel. The end of the leash is then attached to the hawk's block or bow ring via the falconer's knot.

Whichever type of leash is used by the falconer for securing his hawk, at least one spare should be kept at all times so that, in the event of loss of, or damage to, the leash, the falconer can replace it without risking the well-being of his hawk.

A hybrid leash secured to the hawk's swivel.

GLOVE OR GAUNTLET

When I first started in my falconry career, in 1964, I found it impossible to obtain a 'proper' falconry glove and, not having the necessary skills to make my own, I persuaded my father to obtain one from a family friend. I thus flew my hawks wearing a welder's glove.

Today, at the click of a mouse, one can obtain many different types of falconry glove, in different styles, materials, thicknesses and lengths. For a novice falconer, it is worth obtaining guidance from the mentor on which style, length and material is best, although a certain amount of personal preference should be tolerated and encouraged. A glove which is too thick will be cumbersome, while another which is too thin will result in painful experiences when handling the larger and more aggressive hawks. Some falconers like tassels on their gloves, while others decry them. A strong ring, affixed near to the cuff of the glove is essential, as it is to this that the hawk is always fastened when it is being carried by the falconer.

Whichever type of glove is chosen, it will require regular attention to ensure it is kept in good condition. At the end of the day, one will find the glove covered in down, small pieces of meat, blood and egg yolk, and this should be removed by brushing the glove vigorously with a suede brush (i.e. a brush designed to clean suede leather); never use a knife as this will soon ruin the glove. Once the solids are removed, a wipe with a cloth dampened with mildly soapy water will give a clean surface. However, such cleaning will remove the natural oils from the glove and so, once a week, the glove should be treated with one of the many proprietary brands of leather treatment available from falconry furniture manufacturers or saddlery outlets. Do not use this leather treatment in excess, and ensure that any surplus is removed from the glove, which should then be hung up in a warm, dry place overnight.

HOODS

While many falconers can make hoods for their own hawks, many others cannot. Since an ill-fitting hood is useless, and can even be a danger to the hawk on which it is fitted, I believe it best to leave hood-making to the professionals, and I would recommend that the novice falconer buys a suitable hood from a proficient hood-maker.

Hoods come in a variety of styles, e.g. Bahraini, Dutch, Indian, Anglo-Indian. Some styles are better suited for some species of hawk than are others and so guidance should be sought from the professional hood-maker. It is always worthwhile having several different suitable styles and sizes to try on one's hawk before making the final choice.

While some falconers will only ever use hoods on longwings, we train all of our hawks to take the hood; this helps us when having to carry out work on a hawk, e.g. coping its beak and / or talons, imping feathers, etc.

SWUNG LURE, LINE AND STICK

As mentioned in the chapter on training, a swung lure, although usually associated with longwings, is also essential for properly training shortwings and broadwings.

The 'safe' position; the swivel placed between the falconer's fingers while the hawk is being carried. This prevents the hawk from bating too strongly. Note that the leash must still be secured to the falconer's glove whenever the hawk is carried.

The 'safe' position from the inside of the hand.

There are many different designs available from falconry furniture manufacturers, and some falconers make their own by tying together the wings from the quarry species of their hawk. Whichever design is used, a line, attached to a lure stick, will also be needed. This line should be light but strong, and should be attached via a strong swivel. This swivel need not be of the quality of the swivels used in tethering hawks, but should still be fairly substantial if it is not to fail while the falconer is swinging the lure. The line will need to be carefully wound onto the lure stick, in a figure of eight pattern, to prevent tangling. There is a certain knack in winding the line onto the lure stick, and much practice is needed to be able to do this while, at the same time, holding a hawk on the gloved fist. When winding the lure line onto the stick, it is best to put some tension on the line by placing a foot on the line while winding.

A portion of the hawk's daily feed will need to be affixed to the lure. This is usually done by using a short length of nylon twine securely attached to the lure.

DUMMY BUNNY, LINE AND STICK

Although not used for longwings, a dummy bunny is essential for shortwings and broadwings. The line for the dummy bunny need not be as light as that for the swung lure, but will need to be very strong.

CREANCE

The creance is a long length of light nylon line (approximately 30 metres/100 feet) , wound on a stick in a figure of eight pattern, in order to prevent the line becoming tangled when it is deployed. Winding this length of line, one-handed, onto a stick, while carrying a young and untrained hawk on the gloved fist, really does require some practice to perfect, and it is highly recommended that this practice be carried out, and experience gained, when the falconer does not have to carry such a hawk on his other hand. As with all equipment, the falconer should practice its use when he does not have the extra stresses and strains which go hand in glove with handling a live hawk.

Although most falconry equipment suppliers will fasten the creance line to the stick prior to selling it, I strongly recommend that every falconer checks that the creance line is securely attached to the creance stick *before* using the creance. A hawk trailing 30 metres (100 feet) of creance will not survive for long in the wild.

BELLS

When I first started my falconry career, every falconer was expected to use either a very inferior bell, of the type sold for attaching to the collar of a pet cat, or else make his own. Today, there is a plethora of excellent bell manufacturers, but the falconer is strongly advised to look at a wide range before deciding on which type he favours, and will thus fit on his hawks.

There seems to be two schools of thought on the quality of bells used in falconry. One school favours using cheap bells, and discarding and replacing them every season, while the other school favours fitting top quality (and therefore more expensive) bells, which should last for several years. I favour the latter. When a hawk is lost, even when fitted with telemetry (see later in this chapter for more details), a bell is essential for locating the errant hawk, and I would not want to compromise on the quality of equipment needed to recover my hawk.

A bell is normally fitted to the hawk's train (tail), on its two central feathers (known as 'deck feathers'). By fitting the bell on the hawk's train, it will sound more often as the train will move when the bird is flying, when it is perching in a tree and also when it is feeding on the ground (as the hawk bows to grab food, tears it off and then stands up to swallow the food).

However, when the hawk has lost its deck feathers, e.g. when flying a hawk through its moult, then a bell can be affixed to the hawk's leg, usually its aylmeri. It is common for falconers to fit a bell to each leg in such cases. Leg bells, however, are not ideal, as they tend to catch in undergrowth, etc. and will not sound when the hawk is standing or sitting as it is not moving its legs. Even when the hawk is feeding on the ground, it tends not to move its feet much, and any sound made by the bells will be muted by the grass in which the hawk is standing.

When choosing a bell (and it is always best to obtain at least one spare bell), the falconer should listen to the sound and choose the bell making the sound which appeals best to the falconer, since it will be he who needs to be able to hear the bell, if it is to serve its purpose. I particularly favour bells where the ball inside the bell is made from cut glass, as this gives a very high, sharp note which, to my ears, carries further and better than other types.

BATHS

A hawk's bath serves two purposes – to allow the hawk to bathe and also to provide water from which the hawk can drink. I do not agree with those falconers who state that any gravel tray, washing-up bowl or similar will suffice for a hawk's bath. My hawks work hard for me and I believe that they deserve good quality equipment and treatment, and I certainly do not begrudge spending a little extra money to obtain a better piece of equipment for the hawks in my charge.

All good falconry equipment manufacturers will make hawk baths, and there are several different designs. The size of the bath should be such that the hawk can, if it so wishes, be able to get its shoulders under water while bathing. On the principle that a large bath is suitable for a small hawk, while a small bath is not suitable for a large hawk, I recommend that the falconer obtain a hawk bath of a minimum of 750 mm (about 30 inches) in diameter. The bath should be cleaned and refilled on a daily basis.

HAWKING BAG, VEST, WAISTCOAT OR JACKET

Used to carry the hawk's feed, lures, whistles, knife, captured quarry, etc., a hawking bag (or similar) is essential equipment for the falconer. Traditionally, falconers carried a large bag either attached to the belt or carried around the neck and over one shoulder on a strap, the bag hanging down on the falconer's thigh. Although these bags are picturesque and hold much nostalgia for many falconers, they are not the most practical of items. Here at The National Falconry School, we only use such bags when we are giving displays, as they do have appeal for the general public. However, when hawking, i.e. using our hawks for true falconry purposes (i.e. catching live quarry), we use other devices. Some of our staff favour a waistcoat, usually made from waxed material, and which has been modified and altered to their own needs. I use a hawking vest, purpose-made for falconry, and which I jokingly refer to as a 'Swiss Army Bra', since it is used to carry almost everything I require on a hawking day. (See photo adjacent).

A falconer securing a male Harris' hawk to his hawking vest, prior to moving the hawk from the weathering to the mews.

Some falconers use normal jackets, often of waxed material (e.g. the 'Barbour' type), which have been modified for their new use.

Whichever type of bag or jacket a falconer uses, it should have a removable 'meat pocket': this is simply a liner of waterproof material, which fixes in a suitable pocket of the bag or coat, usually via Velcro or press studs. This meat pocket should be thoroughly washed at the end of every day, since it will quickly become soiled with blood, bits of meat and similar fly-attracting material. If not kept clean, the meat pocket can become a prime source of food poisoning for the hawks.

TELEMETRY

Every sensible and thoughtful falconer will use telemetry on his hawks. Without such equipment, recovery of a lost hawk is made extremely difficult, if not impossible.

Unfortunately, some falconers will penny-pinch and justify their decision not to use telemetry by stating that they have either never lost a hawk, or that the species they are flying never becomes lost – both of these statements are untrue. Any falconer who states that he has never lost a hawk, i.e. has never had a hawk which did not return to him when he called it, is stretching the truth. Even the species most described as being 'impossible to lose' (the Harris' hawk) can still become lost. If any reader doubts this statement, a look at the website of the Independent Bird Register (IBR) will persuade him otherwise.

Telemetry is, therefore an essential for the true falconer.

Pill boxes used for storing the small batteries used for telemetry for both hawks and ferrets.

There are various designs of telemetry and, in various parts of the world, these operate on different frequencies. It is, however, still possible to purchase telemetry sets which operate on illegal frequencies and so the axiom *caveat emptor* (buyer beware) is worth bearing in mind. It is also worth remembering that frequencies allotted as legal for this type of radio system may be changed by the government of the day. I suggest that you contact your own legislators for the definitive answer on this.

Where telemetry is used, the transmitter(s) must be affixed to the hawk in a manner in which they can operate, but whereby they do not interfere with the hawk's flying etc. Normally these transmitters are fixed in the hawk's train (tail) but when in moult they may be fixed on the hawk's leg.

Never fly a hawk without fitting new batteries to its telemetry. I have known falconers who, perhaps wanting to save a little money and perhaps also believing that the hawk in question did not really require telemetry, have flown their hawks with older, used batteries. Of course, on most occasions the falconer will not need to use the telemetry to get back his hawk, but on the one occasion when it is needed, it is a very sad and frustrated falconer who discovers that the batteries in the hawk's transmitter have failed. It is simply not worth the risk to use old batteries.

The receiver section of the telemetry will require an antenna (aerial) to pick up the signals from the transmitter, and the most commonly used type is the yagi. This is a directional aerial which is attached to the receiver via a length of coaxial cable, and there are various designs for different uses, ranges, etc.

It is always advisable for the falconer to keep the yagi with him while hawking, rather than leaving it in the car, and a suitable carry case should be acquired for this purpose. Likewise, all of the telemetry equipment – transmitters, transmitter mounts, batteries, receiver, testing equipment, small tool kit, etc., should be stored safely in a secure box, which should be easily available at all times to the falconer.

LEATHER, ETC

There are many types of 'leather' in use by falconers today, including calf, buckskin and kangaroo skin. Each type has its adherents, and it is worth looking at the range, finding out the advantages and disadvantages of each, before buying large amounts. When working with leather, it should be noted that skins have a grain, and this will give the skin differing qualities, dependent on which way the grain runs. A good falconry course will explain these idiosyncrasies to the tyro.

LEATHER-WORKING TOOLS

If the falconer is to make, repair or adjust any falconry furniture, he will require a small set of leather-working tools, as listed below:

Scalpel

Get a couple of different sizes, and with replaceable blades. Once a blade loses its edge, change it; blunt blades lead to far more cuts and injuries than do sharp blades.

Safety Rule

A special steel rule, designed to minimise the risk of injury while using it with a scalpel.

Hole Punches

Two types of these punches are needed – rotary and wad punches. Rotary punches are used for making small holes in leather, e.g. when making the traditional jesses, while wad punches are required for making large holes, such as those in the aylmeri into which will be fitted eyelets. Both types will require ongoing maintenance to ensure their effective use, i.e. they will require sharpening and care when using.

Eyelet Tool

Used to fit eyelets to aylmeri, jackets, etc. As eyelets come in a range of sizes to suit different uses, the falconer will need tools of the correct size to match the eyelets being used.

PERCHES

BLOCK PERCH

Traditionally, longwings are given blocks perches, although I know of several falconers who, having discovered that their longwing is happier on a bow perch, have successfully gone contrary to this tradition. As a hawk may spend many hours on its perch, it is imperative that the perch is suitable and kept scrupulously clean. Where a hawk is kept on an unsuitable and/or dirty perch, it will almost certainly fall prey to 'bumblefoot', a condition of the feet which can lead to the need for amputation.

A block should be big enough for the hawk to sit on without having to stand on its own toes, while also preventing it from straddling the block. The block's surface should be covered with a material which is waterproof, easy to clean, comfortable for the hawk and has a roughened surface to allow the hawk to gain purchase. Some falconers use leather, which is easy to work, but which will absorb large quantities of moisture and bacteria, and is very difficult to clean properly. Others favour Astroturf, which does not soak up water, allows air to circulate around the hawk's feet and is easy to work. However, the base of the nylon/plastic 'grass' tends to allow the build-

A gyr x saker hybrid tiercel

up of all kinds of detritus, and can easily harbour large numbers of potentially harmful pathogens.

We only use perches covered with specially designed and moulded rubber tops. The initial designs for this type of perch were made by Jim Moss (Crown Falconry – see Appendix 3 for more details) and, although now copied and imitated by other falconry furniture manufacturers, I still believe that Jim's rubber-topped blocks and bows are the best.

BOW PERCH

Shortwings and broadwings, on the whole, tend to prefer to perch on bows, rather than on blocks. A bow needs an adequate surface for the hawk, as detailed above, and the bow should be high enough off the ground to ensure that the hawk does not damage its train when using the perch.

While some bow perches are designed with spikes to push into the ground on the weathering lawn, others, described as 'portable' have large, heavy feet, making them capable of being used both indoors and outdoors. However, caution must be exercised with these portable bows, since large hawks can move them. The better designed portable bow perches have holes drilled through the feet, through which pegs can be pushed into the ground when using them outside, which will prevent the hawk from moving the bow.

OTHER NECESSARY EQUIPMENT

NAIL CLIPPERS

Nail clippers are used to clip a hawk's talons, and also to trim its beak to length, before the beak is shaped by a falconer using a set of small coping files. *Never* use scissors or implements with a scissor action for these purposes, as they can easily cause damage and pain to the hawk.

COPING FILES

Sold to engineers as needle files, a set will consist of several different shapes, most of which the falconer will find extremely useful when shortening and shaping (i.e. coping) a hawk's beak.

WHISTLE

Used to recall a hawk, most types of whistle will serve this purpose, as long as the hawk is trained to that type. A wise falconer will fasten the whistle to his bag, vest or similar object, via a lanyard or similar, to prevent the whistle's loss during hawking forays.

KNIFE

Some falconers prefer a folding knife, while others favour a fixed blade (or sheath) knife. The blade should be kept clean and sharp, and care should be taken never to place a knife on the ground, as this will inevitably lead to its loss.

Many falconers favour a knife with a rounded blade and sharp point, for despatching wounded quarry, without the danger of an eager hawk grabbing a sharpened blade with its feet, which will then sustain serious injuries.

BEWITS

A bewit is simply a small strip of leather, or similar, and is used for tying items such as bells to the hawk. Today, most falconers use nylon cable ties (see below), although these should never be used to fasten directly onto the hawk's legs, etc., as they can cause abrasions.

CABLE TIES

The ubiquitous nylon cable tie has a myriad of uses in modern falconry, but should never be used directly on the skin/flesh of a hawk, as this could cause abrasion wounds.

A selection of sizes, widths and lengths should be obtained. Electronic equipment suppliers can also furnish tools designed to tighten these ties and trim off the excess length at the same time.

ID TAGS

While many falconers fly hawks fitted with closed rings on which there is a contact telephone number, for those who do not, small metal tags, engraved with the falconer's contact details, can be used. They should be fitted to the hawk by a method, and in a position, whereby they do not interfere with the hawk's functions nor impair its safety and well-being.

CHAPTER 7
FITNESS TRAINING THE HAWK

In order to perform its job properly, a hawk – of any kind – will need to be fit. In the wild, hawks would gain this fitness in the natural course of their life and the activities in which they would naturally indulge. However, in captivity, it is down to the falconer to ensure that every hawk under his control is given ample opportunities to gain fitness. Although a commonly held belief, it is not good enough to hope that a hawk will gain fitness by chasing wild quarry. As the unfit hawk is highly unlikely to catch its quarry, it will start to lose heart – failure always breeds failure. The better course of action is to get the hawk fit before it is allowed to hunt. In that way, the hawk may well catch its quarry and success will breed more success.

Each species of hawk, and even individual hawks, will have its own difficulties in obtaining fitness, but we can generalise. Accipiters tend to gain fitness fairly easily, while buteos (and also the Parabuteo – the Harris' hawk) will require a lot of work and effort from a dedicated falconer to get them really fit, while longwinged hawks can be made fit fairly easily.

Daily workout sessions are required for any hawk to become really fit, and the falconer must ensure that he has allocated and allowed ample time for this. It is also important that the falconer thinks about what activities will get the hawk fit – simply casting off the hawk and recalling it will not produce a fit hawk. Most flights like this involve the hawk simply gliding and putting in very little effort, and so the falconer must think what work he can give the hawk which will produce the required level of fitness.

ACCIPITERS AND BUTEOS (Including the Harris' Hawk)

As mentioned earlier, accipiters have a natural *joie de vivre* and almost seem to want to get fit. Simply giving them regular opportunities to fly will almost certainly produce fit hawks. If a falconer can fly his hawk over hilly country, fitness for the hawk can be achieved more easily than flying the hawk over flat country. When a falconer casts off his hawk and then calls it to him while the falconer is standing uphill of the hawk, the hawk will need to make much more effort than it would need for a simple straight flight, and thus this will produce a higher level of fitness in the hawk in much less time than may be needed otherwise.

DUMMY BUNNY

Use of the dummy bunny can also result in heightened levels of fitness, if this lure is used correctly. By placing dummy bunnies in cover along the intended route the falconer will take when exercising his hawk *before* setting out with the hawk, opportunities will be given to the hawk to chase an unexpected quarry. All that is required is that the falconer, with the hawk lofted well away from him, pick up the lure handle and run away from the hawk, while dragging the dummy bunny. We have extended this idea, and use various dummy bunnies on each such hawk exercising/training walk. These dummy bunnies are a combination of the normal type, i.e. lures on the end of a line which in turn is secured to the lure handle, while others are attached to a winch. These winches are well hidden in the undergrowth, and have extremely long lines (up to 100 metres/110 yards) leading to the dummy bunnies. Each line to a dummy bunny is taken across the field, and placed around pegs which have been firmly driven into the ground. These pegs act as pulleys, and once the winch has been activated (by a radio control device carried by the falconer), the dummy bunny keeps changing direction, as would a real rabbit. By carefully turning the winch on and then off, the falconer can control the speed at which the dummy bunny travels across the field, making it extremely realistic.

Along the route of the lure line, we have placed several 'hides', which consist of piping or heavy wooden boxes, and these simulate the bolt holes that would be used by real rabbits. With a little imagination, there is no limit as to the challenges a falconer can build for his hawk.

SWING LURE

For shortwings, broadwings and longwings, a swung lure can, and should, be used to call the hawk and give it exercise. With longwings, the hawk is worked hard and made to chase the lure, which is only served when the falconer believes that his hawk has worked hard. This can be a very fine line, as if the hawk is not worked hard, it will not get fit, but if the falconer attempts to work the hawk too hard, the hawk can (and usually does) work out that it can pitch (land) in a suitable tree to regain its breath and composure, before beginning its assault again. Such a hawk will never really push itself, and will never gain top fitness. When a longwing pitches in a tree or on a building, outcrop, etc., the falconer should ensure that he never serves the lure as the longwing takes off from its perch to attack the lure. At the very least, the hawk should be made to do two or three passes before being given the lure.

In order to ensure that the hawk does not make a habit of this frustrating action, the falconer should fly it in different locations and, if possible, in areas where there are no suitable perches.

As the longwing is flown to the swung lure, the falconer should watch its beak. As in humans, when working hard, the hawk's mouth begins to gape in an effort to take in more oxygen. The trick is to know when the hawk has worked hard enough, and this can only come through experience.

With a shortwing or broadwing, the swung lure should be used to call the hawk to the falconer, and then served for the hawk as it comes in to the falconer. At first, this will simply mean dropping the lure on the floor ahead of the hawk but, as the hawk becomes fitter, the lure can be flung as high as possible, making the hawk power up hard to catch it. Whichever style is used, the falconer should never let go of the lure handle. A hawk which catches a lure which is not held, may well fly with it, and this can have serious consequences, as the line and handle can become tangled in trees, on buildings or even on power lines. A dead hawk may well result from allowing it to fly while trailing a lure line.

CIRCUIT TRAINING

If a human wishes to get fit, he may well resort to attending a gymnasium, where he will carry out many exercises. This is often referred to as circuit training and is the basis we use for getting our hawks fit, especially after the moult.

During the moult, we place our hawks in large aviaries and feed them quite large quantities of high calorie, high protein, high calcium feed: without such a diet, the hawks will not grow good strong new feathers to replace their old ones. An undesirable consequence of this, however, is that the hawks will become fat (i.e. in high condition) and unfit. When the moult is completed (about 14 to 16 weeks), the hawks will need to be 'reclaimed' (manned and retrained), and then their fitness must be built up. While it is possible to get a hawk fit through the methods already described, we have found much better methods which result in our hawks becoming much fitter in less time.

Once a hawk has been manned and is flying free, we encourage it to jump vertically from the ground (or its block/bow) to the falconer's glove, where food is waiting. Once the hawk accepts this new practice, we start to make the reward (i.e. the feed) much less predictable, i.e. we only put food on the fist about every three or four jumps, but never in any particular sequence. More practise with the hawk follows, until the hawk can easily jump ten to fifteen times to the fist held about a metre (39 inches) above it, and then we go on to the next stage. As the hawk jumps to the fist, the falconer raises his fist to shoulder height (about 1½ metres/5 feet); this causes the hawk to have to make much more effort than before, and increases its fitness level. After a few sessions (we usually give three sessions in any one day at this stage in a hawk's fitness training), the exercise is repeated, but this time the falconer raises his gloved hand as high as he can (i.e. about 2 metres/6½ feet), again as the hawk jumps. Once the hawk can manage twenty to thirty such jumps, we raise the whole thing by using a step ladder. In each training session, provided the preceding sessions have gone according to plan and the hawk is managing its exercises, the falconer goes up one rung of the step ladder, until he is at the highest point at which he feels safe and confident.

To make the exercise even more challenging for the hawk, it can be carried out with the hawk tethered via a length of fine chain, such as that used for bath plugs. The end of this chain must, of course, be securely fastened to a safe anchor point. As the hawk jumps higher, the weight it is carrying will increase exponentially, i.e. the higher the hawk jumps, the more weight it carries. The hawk's fitness will increase at a phenomenally fast rate when it is exercised like this, and it can be easily made ready for the hunting season.

As with all training, a little imagination is required from the trainer, and the exercises should never be overdone. Little and often should be the maxim. Repeating the same exercises *ad nauseum* will simply result in a bored hawk which will soon show its displeasure by refusing to carry out the exercises or, at the very least, only do the work half-heartedly.

CHAPTER 8
FIELD TACTICS

In order to hunt any species, it is essential to know as much as possible about the natural history of one's intended quarry and, in particular, its habits. Different hawks can be used to hunt different species, with some being suited to hunt almost all those detailed below, while others have only specialist uses. Another influence on the quarry which one can hunt with a hawk, is the type of country available. Although a female peregrine may well be suitable for hunting many feathered species of quarry, it would be a pointless exercise to try to fly her through heavily wooded country. Not everyone is lucky enough to have access to hundreds of acres of open moorland on which they can fly their longwinged hawks.

RABBITS

The rabbit (*Oryctolagus cuniculus*) is arguably the mainstay of an austringer's (i.e. a falconer who flies only broadwings and shortwings) hunting activities and, in many areas of the world, rabbits are present in pest-like numbers. In the UK, it is estimated that, in 2006, there was a rabbit population in excess of 45 million, according to the UK's Department for Environment, Food and Rural Affairs (Defra).

Probably introduced into mainland Britain by the Normans about 800 years ago, the rabbits were not technically wild, as they were confined to managed warrens (managed by warreners), and were mainly in coastal areas of the country. Rabbit meat was a well established commodity by the fourteenth century, reaching a peak around the beginning of the nineteenth century. Fifty years later, the economic value of rabbits and their produce – meat and skins – had declined and the rabbit had become an agricultural pest.

In October 1953, a few English farmers introduced several rabbits, bought in and brought from France to farmland around the English village of Edenbridge, Kent. These rabbits were infected with the disease myxomatosis and, on 13 October 1953, the UK Government officially announced that the country had an outbreak of the disease. At the time, the rabbit population in the UK was estimated at about 100 million and, within six months, this population had been reduced by 99%, thanks to the ravages of myxomatosis. Since this time, many rabbits have developed a degree of immunity to myxomatosis, although the disease does still exist and, in some areas, can wipe out whole populations of rabbits. Rabbits which have had the disease and recovered from it, can easily be identified by the scarring of the tissues around the animal's eyes.

Myxomatosis was originally found in the Tapeti, the Brazilian or forest rabbit (*Sylvilagus brasiliensis*), a cottontail rabbit species found in Central and South America, to which the disease is not fatal. Scientists cultivated the disease in laboratories and in mid-1952, released rabbits infected with myxomatosis into the suburbs of Paris, where rabbits were doing immense damage to the gardens and parks of the area. Within a few weeks, the disease had spread throughout France, and it is probably from these diseased rabbits that the farmers of Edenbridge obtained the rabbits which were released – seemingly with the blessing of the UK authorities – into England later that same year.

Rabbits are commonly found in short grass habitats on heaths and agricultural land, where they graze the areas closer to the ground than sheep. As rabbits graze all year round, with the most severe impacts in the winter, rabbits cause more damage to agricultural crops than any other pest species in the UK, and so are widely regarded as the number one agricultural pest.

Rabbits are mainly active grazers at dawn and dusk, i.e. crepuscular, although in undisturbed areas some may graze close to their burrows during the day. Rabbits eat a wide variety of plants, but have a particular taste for young succulent leaves and shoots.

The breeding season for rabbits is mainly from January to June, although for the last fifteen years, I have seen evidence of rabbit breeding – young kittens, milky does, etc. – throughout the year. With an average litter size of between three and seven kittens, and litters produced at intervals of just thirty days, the rabbit population has the potential to grow at a phenomenal rate. It is very common for does (females) to be mated within hours of giving birth.

Only one adult buck (male) rabbit is allowed within the confines of the family burrow, and young bucks reaching sexual maturity are attacked and chased off by the alpha buck. As a doe becomes pregnant, she will select a place in one of the tunnels, where she will dig out a small excavation, line it with fur pulled from her stomach, and give birth. Within thirty to forty minutes of giving birth, the doe will have walled in the young kittens (which are naked, deaf and blind at this stage), and will only return to the nest two to three times each day, and stay for no more than twenty to thirty minutes. As the kittens become more mobile, the wall will become broken down, and the kittens will no longer stay in the area, but move throughout the warren, and even venture outside.

For a falconer to hunt rabbits, he will require the help of a few ferrets (see Chapter 5 for more details), and a dog if he wants to flush the conies from the grasslands, under bushes, etc. The hawks used must be used to working with these other species, as must the falconer. It is good practice to have one member of the hunting team tasked with working the hawk, another with the dogs and yet another with the ferrets, in order to ensure good sport and the health and welfare of all concerned.

When approaching the rabbit's warren, silence must be maintained if the inhabitants of the warren are not to be warned of danger. Any unusual noise, sight or even the smell of tobacco can, and usually does, frighten rabbits enough to discourage them from bolting from their subterranean refuge. Using his eyes, the falconer should seek evidence of rabbit activity – fresh scrapes, paw prints and droppings, etc. If there are no fresh droppings, and the holes to the warren are full of leaves and have cobwebs in them, then there are obviously no rabbits there and it is best to look for another warren.

If the falconer and his team discover evidence of recent rabbit activity, then the hawk(s) should be quietly removed from the carrying boxes and made ready for flying; telemetry should be affixed to every hawk involved in this type of work. When the hawks are ready, the falconer must decide if he is to fly the hawks from his fist, or to loft them – cast the hawks into trees, where they will 'take stand' or wait until they see the rabbits, which they will then chase. If the decision is to loft the hawks, this should be done so that the hawks are in a position downwind of the warren, high up and giving them a good view of the exits from the warren. If the hawks are to be flown off the fist, the falconers must position themselves downwind of the warren, and hold the hawks so that they can see any rabbits which bolt from the warren.

Once the falconers are in place, the ferrets are placed at the mouths of the tunnels; each ferret will be fitted with a transmitter collar to enable it to be tracked underground or retrieved if the ferret does not – or cannot – exit the warren of its own accord.

When a rabbit bolts from the warren, the ferret may be very close behind, and so the hawk must not be slipped (released) until the falconer can see that the rabbit is free from the constraints of the warren, and the ferret is not chasing it. At this point, the falconer should whistle or shout 'Ho!', to signal to both the hawks and the human members of the team that a rabbit is running, and the hawks, if held on the fist, should be cast in the direction of the bolting coney.

An immature hawk, chasing one of its first rabbits, may make the mistake of grabbing at and binding to the rabbit's backside. If it does so, then the rabbit is likely to continue to run, although impeded by the hawk's weight. If it is a strong rabbit, it may run quite a distance, dragging the forlorn hawk after it, and often causing damage to the hawk's feathers. If the hawk can get a purchase on the ground, then the rabbit will be held, but will still continue to kick out, and this may also damage the hawk. It is vital that the falconer bears these facts in mind at all times and, when he sees the hawk strike the rabbit, the falconer should run towards the pair to give aid to the hawk, and humanely despatch the rabbit.

Once the falconer has 'killed' the rabbit, it is sensible to check that the coney really is dead. Over the years I have seen countless 'dead' rabbits suddenly jump up and run off to safety – such rabbits have certainly not been killed. To check on whether a rabbit is dead, one has simply to touch the animal's eyes: if the rabbit blinks, it is not

A cast (two) of male Harris' hawks taking stand near to a rabbit warren. (*Photo: Nick Ridley*)

dead; if it does not blink, it is dead. If possible, the falconer should kill the rabbit with a knife while the hawk is holding the coney. Great care must be taken to ensure that the hawk does not grab at the knife, as it will seriously damage its toes and foot if allowed to do so. Some falconers, rather than use a normal knife for this, use a screwdriver with a sharpened point. Properly used, this will humanely kill the rabbit but cannot damage the feet of the hawk, should it grab the blade. Never attempt to wrestle a hawk off its kill, as this will cause great resentment between the hawk and the falconer. Where this happens, the hawk in question will always attempt to fly off with its captured prey when it sees the falconer approach.

Once the rabbit is dead, the falconer should cover the rabbit (using his bag, a small towel or similar item), and throw a small piece of food about a metre away from the hawk. On seeing this food, the hawk will usually release its grip on the dead rabbit, which it feels has disappeared, and fly to the food. While the hawk is distracted with the food, the falconer must quickly, and without any fuss, retrieve the dead rabbit and place it in the falconer's bag, out of view of the hawk.

HARES

In the UK, there are two species of hare; the common, or brown hare (*Lepus europaeus*) and the blue or mountain hare (*Lepus timidus*). In Ireland, the latter is known as the Irish hare. The brown hare is to be found on low ground, while the blue is found in some regions of mountain and moorland. In winter, the coat of the blue hare will turn to white, as an aid to camouflage. Hares have longer limbs than rabbits, and can run much faster.

THE BLUE HARE

Considerably smaller than the brown hare, the blue hare has a more rounded shape and, unlike the brown hare, this species does not have a black upper surface on its tail. The blue hare also has shorter ears and legs than does the brown hare. In summer, blue hares have a grey/black coat and moult twice a year, once in late autumn and then again in the spring when they lose their thick winter coat. The blue hare has a head and body length of about 500 to 600 mm (20 to 24 inches), and weighs about 2 ½ to 4 kg (6 to 9 lbs).

Blue hares graze on grasses, heather, bilberry, gorse, juniper, herbs and various farm crops, and are normally solitary. When the weather is severe, or when there is an exceptionally rich food supply in a specific area, blue hares have been known to congregate in large groups of over seventy animals. Although they normally live on the surface, in a 'form' (a depression in the ground), under the cover of rock outcrops or heather, in extremely cold conditions and in areas of deep snow, blue hares will burrow for shelter. They have a range of between 80 and 100 hectares (200 – 250 acres). Mountain hares can reach speeds of over 60 kph (38 mph) when threatened. Blue hares have a gestation period (pregnancy) of about fifty days, with a breeding season from February to September, and their litters consist of between one and five young (known as leverets). Young blue hares are precocial, i.e. they are born with fur and eyes and ears open, and the leverets are weaned at three weeks.

THE BROWN HARE

This hare is larger than the European rabbit with a head and body length of between 480 to 700 mm (19 to 28 inches); the brown hare weighs between 3 and 5 kilos (6½ and 11 pounds). With its long limbs, the brown hare has a loping gait when running. The black-tipped ears of the brown hare are about as long as the hare's head, and the brown hare holds down its tail, which has a black upper surface, when the animal is running. The brown hare moults in spring and autumn, and its summer coat is slightly lighter than its winter coat, which has a reddish tinge.

Brown hares are widespread throughout the UK, except in the north-western areas of Scotland, and it is thought that they were brought to the UK from Asia, by the Romans. Introduced into Ireland for sport in the nineteenth century, it is believed that the spread of the brown hare has been checked in that country due to competition from the Irish hare.

Feeding mainly on herbs in the summer, grasses in the winter, and also cereal and root crops when they can get them, the favoured habitat of the brown hare is temperate open country. This species is found in flat country among open grassland and arable farms, using woodland and hedgerows as daytime rest areas. Brown hares are not particularly aggressive, and although an adult brown hare may occupy a range of almost 300 hectares (750 acres), it may well share this territory with other brown hares.

During the breeding season, March to August, the brown hare's courtship involves boxing, and this is where we get the expression the 'mad March hare'. Although often thought to be part of the species' mating ritual between the sexes, this is actually unreceptive females fending off males. Brown hares can have up to three litters of four, after a gestation period of about forty-two days, and the leverets are weaned after a month.

Although the blue hare can be hunted by many of the hawks flown by modern falconers, the brown hare is much larger than the rabbit, and can only really be hunted with the large broadwings and shortwings, such as female Harris' hawks, goshawks and eagles.

A well-trained dog is essential for hunting hares: it is their job to find the hares, enabling the falconer to slip his hawk. Pointers and similar breeds will simply mark the area where a hare is sitting, while spaniels will spring (flush) the hare for the waiting hawk. As with the rabbit, immature hawks may make the mistake of grabbing at and binding to the animal's backside, allowing the hare to continue to run, although impeded by the hawk's weight. A hare can run quite a distance with a hawk attached, and the hawk will almost certainly be injured if this is allowed to happen. If the hawk is lucky enough to be able to get a purchase on the ground as it is being pulled along, then the hare may be held, but is still likely to continue to kick out, damaging the hawk. It is vital that the falconer bears these facts in mind at all times and, when he sees the hawk strike the hare, the falconer should run towards the pair to humanely despatch the animal, while at the same time protecting the hawk from injury from the hare's flailing feet.

Hares need to be checked before being pronounced dead by the falconer. This is easily done by touching the hare's eyes with a finger tip – if it blinks, it is not dead, if it does not blink, it is dead. As with a captured rabbit, the falconer should kill the hare with a knife while the hawk is holding its quarry, taking care not to allow the hawk to grab the blade of the knife.

Once the hare is dead, the falconer should cover it (using his bag, a small towel or similar item) thus hiding it from the hawk's gaze, and at the same time throw a small piece of food about a metre away from the hawk. On seeing this food, the hawk should release its grip on the dead hare and fly to the piece of food thrown by the falconer. While the hawk is thus distracted, the falconer can quickly retrieve the dead animal and place it in his bag for transport home.

PHEASANT

Pheasants (*Phasianus colchicus*) can be either easy quarry or an extremely difficult challenge for a hawk. In the UK, pheasants are bred and released on shoots and similar areas; obviously some pheasants will breed in the wild, but in most places these will be in the minority. At the start of the hunting (shooting) season, the pheasants will be fairly unfit and quite naïve, and only fly the absolute minimum distance that they need to. As the season progresses, so too do the pheasants. They begin flying much better, being fitter and far more experienced than they were at the beginning of the season.

With most chases from broadwings and shortwings, the hawk will give chase when it sees the pheasant running along the ground, although as the distance between hunter and hunted reduces, the pheasant will take to its wings. The pheasant's strategy often leaves a bewildered hawk sitting on the ground where the pheasant had just been, while the pheasant itself is flying away with far too much of a lead for the hawk to catch it. If a cast (two) of hawks is flown at such a bird, there is the possibility that the second hawk could take the pheasant, but usually, the pheasant escapes unscathed. As the hawk gets fitter and more experienced, it may be able to recover from its initial failure and take off at once, its feet having hardly touched the ground.

When a pheasant is missed by the hawk's first attempt, it will fly away a short distance and then put in to cover. Some hawks, on seeing this, will crash straight into the cover, while others will throw up and take stand on a tree branch overlooking the pheasant's cover. The falconer should be ready, in the latter instance, to reflush the pheasant, either with his dog or do the job himself. A hawk thus primed and with adrenalin coursing through its veins, is unlikely to miss its second opportunity.

If the falconer sees a pheasant sitting tightly on the ground, he should loft his hawk on a nearby tree branch, and then flush the pheasant towards the waiting hawk. Goshawks take to such hunting very easily, while broadwings will need to be very fit and experienced before excelling at such sport.

PARTRIDGE

One of the most prized of all game birds for the falconer, the partridge is a very difficult bird for a hawk to catch.

In the UK there are currently two species of partridge: the English or grey partridge (*Perdix perdix*) and the French or red-legged partridge (*Alectoris rufa*). The English partridge is smaller, slighter and takes flight more readily than its larger French cousin. Both species are regularly encountered and both are flushed by walking up or the use of a well trained dog, and both spend most of their time in groups known as coveys, which may vary from a half a dozen to almost a hundred.

Even with the best of luck, it will still take a very fit and experienced hawk to take a mature partridge, and it will also have to have a dogged determination. A hawk – either longwinged or shortwinged – may take a partridge on the wing, but most shortwings will only manage one which has put in to cover. Buteos and Harris' hawks will only manage a partridge if they can ambush the bird before it gets flying strongly.

GROUSE

There are relatively few falconers who can regularly fly their longwinged hawk at grouse, and this part of the sport is considered by most to be the pinnacle of the sport, producing the most difficult challenges with the most rewarding results. As grouse are fairly large birds, the hawks flown at them must also be large; the tiercel peregrine is, on the whole, too small for this task, although male peregrine x gyr falcon or saker hybrid falcons can be large enough to take on this formidable quarry.

Whichever hawk is used, it must be able to wait on, and this is a skill which will only come with the hawk's experiential learning, gained through both failure and success. When I first started in falconry, I believed that a hawk was taught to wait on by hiding the lure, which would then be served when the hawk was in position. Unfortunately, this is not the case as, when the lure disappears, the hawk simply waits for it to reappear, and circles around the falconer while doing so.

Grouse hawking cannot take place without a couple of good hawking dogs. Humans can walk past innumerable grouse, while they lie hidden in the heather but a good dog, usually a well trained pointer or setter, will pick up the scent of the grouse, and then move into a position where it feels confident enough to mark it by pointing. At that stage, and when the dog has settled into a good, positive point, the falconer unhoods the hawk, and allows it to rouse, mute and generally prepare itself for the flight, at which time the falconer will cast the hawk into the sky, into the wind. As the hawk mounts to its correct pitch, its mere presence will frighten the grouse enough to ensure that it will not move. The falconer carefully and slowly moves until he is standing downwind of the hawk, and between the dog and the grouse, but upwind of the grouse, at which time the falconer calls his hawk towards him. As the hawk reaches its pitch and turns into the wind, the falconer must give the order to the dog to flush the grouse.

As the grouse takes off downwind, the falcon will stoop on it, rapidly gaining on the grouse until the hawk can grab the bird (bind). Then the hawk, still holding the grouse, will turn into the wind to reduce its speed and land with the grouse in its feet.

ROOK

The quarry of only the longwings, rooks make for a challenging sport, and a hawk flown at these corvids must be trained to fly out of the hood. During training with the lure, the hawk should be held by one person, while the falconer begins swinging the lure. In this way, as soon as the hood is removed, the hawk sees the lure and will immediately take off to chase it. Rook hawks must also be extremely fit, and this fitness is gained by making them work hard with the swung lure.

When a rook is being chased, it will instinctively head downwind in order to prevent the hawk from using the wind to get into an advantageous position above it. The rook will also head into any bit of cover it can find, knowing that longwings cannot manoeuvre in such places, while at the same time taking every opportunity to dodge, weave, twist and generally frustrate the attempts of the longwing to catch it.

To give the novice longwinged hawk a good chance of success, it should be slipped at a small flock of rooks – not fewer than two rooks and no more than four – and at a reasonable distance (about 40 to 50 metres / 130 to 160 feet), and always into the wind, with the rooks airborne. Too few rooks, and the hawk may not be able to get into the correct position; too many and the hawk may literally be stuck for choice and, in its hesitation, allow the rooks to escape.

A good rook hawk is extremely fit and persistent to the point of it being a vice. There is not much more exciting than seeing a good rook hawk in action.

COOT AND MOORHEN

Coots (*Fulica atra*) are the more difficult of these two water birds, as they are bigger and stronger than the diminutive moorhen (*Gallinula chloropus*), but the moorhen is a good choice for entering a novice hawk, and is a challenge worth pursuing for the falconer flying a sparrowhawk.

Both moorhens and coots are usually seen on water, and this can make life difficult for the falconer and his hawk. Never attempt to slip a hawk at one of these birds sitting on water deep enough for them to be able to dive.

DUCK

In the UK, it is usually mallard (*Anas platyrhynchos*) which is hunted, and as with coot and moorhen, these birds should only be attempted when on land. Duck found in the UK can be either wild or those bred to be let out into the wild for hunting purposes, and there is a world of difference between them. Wild duck are easily spooked, and much more difficult to hunt. Duck hunts usually end with both duck and hawk in the water, where a strong hawk will drown its quarry and then make for the shore, using its wings as feathered oars.

GREY SQUIRREL

Although popular quarry with some falconers, I see far too much danger (to the hawk) in hunting grey squirrels (*Sciurus carolinensis*). The bodies of these rodents are long and extremely articulated, and it is all too easy for a squirrel, caught in a hawk's feet, to twist around and bite the hawk, inflicting great damage and injury. In some countries, it is possible to purchase a form of 'chain mail' which can be fastened onto the legs of hawks to give them some protection against the vicious teeth of squirrels, but to me it is simply a risk too far.

LAMPING

A fairly recent innovation in falconry has been to hunt rabbits at night, using a lamp to illuminate the coney for the hawk. Harris' hawks are ideal for this purpose and, once trained, excel at this aspect of the sport.

Once permission has been gained to lamp at night over suitable country, the falconer will require a large, powerful lamp and a suitable battery. The hawk must be trained to hunt by lamplight, and this is best achieved by having a light shone on a dummy bunny as it moves in the dark – we use a darkened barn for this early training. Some falconers recommend sewing reflecting sequins or tape onto the lure to simulate the reflective eyes of the rabbit but we have never bothered with this. Before a hawk is flown at night, its bells should be either removed or taped, to help it approach the intended prey in complete silence. We always fit telemetry to hawks flown at night, along with small, powerful, self-powered LEDs, which help us locate the hawk even in pitch black conditions. We also train the hawk to accept food given on the falconer's fist, when illuminated by the light of a small torch. This allows us to feed the hawk without having a powerful light alerting rabbits to our presence, but also provides us with an easy way of calling the bird to the falconer's fist in the dark.

Another essential when lamping is the aid of a trusted assistant, whose only job will be to walk with the lamp, while the falconer, a few metres to one side, walks with his hawk. It is important that lamping is never tried single-handed, since a hawk flying down a beam of light will blot out the light as it nears the intended prey, thus making it all but impossible for the hawk to take the rabbit.

As the team walks though the field, the lamp is swung left and right until one or more rabbits are seen fairly close to the falconer, at which time the hawk is slipped. The human with the lamp must ensure that the lamp's beam is kept on the rabbit as it runs for safety, and the hawk will head for this coney. If the hawk catches the rabbit, it must be despatched as described earlier in this chapter. If the hawk misses the rabbit, the light should be immediately turned off, which will cause the hawk to drop to the floor. After about ten to fifteen seconds, the falconer can shine his torch onto his glove and the hawk will return.

HAWKING FROM A VEHICLE

This can be carried out in daylight or as part of lamping activities, and helps the falconer cover far more ground. While it is possible to slip the hawk by holding it out of a side window, life is made much easier if the vehicle has a sunroof which allows the falconer to stand, head and shoulders out of the vehicle, with his gloved hand, on which sits the hawk, resting on the vehicle's roof.

CHAPTER 9

FIRST AID AND HEALTH

FIRST AID

Hawks kept in good, clean conditions and fed a properly balanced and nutritious diet of top quality feed are extremely hardy, and will rarely require any medical care. However, hawks used for falconry purposes, by definition of their work, may well sustain injuries. Some of these will be minor and well within the capabilities of the falconer to put right, while others will require the attention of a veterinary surgeon. In some countries, the use of drugs such as antibiotics is rigorously controlled, while in other countries, a far more cavalier attitude is held regarding these drugs. I have deliberately not recommended that the falconer obtain, keep and administer antibiotics to any animal in his care, as I feel this is totally irresponsible. Where treatments *may* require the administration of antibiotics and similar controlled drugs, I recommend that the falconer seek the services of a veterinary surgeon.

THE BASICS OF FIRST AID

First aid is the skilled application of accepted principles of treatment on the occurrence of an accident, or in the case of a sudden illness, using facilities and materials available at the time. The objectives of first aid are threefold:

- To sustain life
- To prevent the patient's condition worsening
- To promote the patient's recovery

When finding an injured hawk, you should attempt to:

- Assess the situation
- Diagnose the condition
- Treat immediately and adequately

ASSESSING THE SITUATION

Keep calm and look at what has happened/is happening. While it is imperative that time is not wasted, it is just as important that you do not act hastily and, in so doing, make matters worse. Wherever possible, the cause of the hawk's pain and/or distress should be taken away from the hawk, rather than the hawk being moved from the pain.

Look for any indications as to the cause of the hawk's problem.
Signs to look for include:

- State of consciousness
- Breathing
- Bleeding
- Fractures
- Shock
- Movement
- Pain

Your priorities must always be:

- Airways
- Breathing
- Circulation

If the hawk is not breathing, the airways must be cleared before any attempt is made to get the hawk breathing. Airways can be blocked by a foreign body, or it could be that the hawk's tongue is blocking its throat. Vomit is another major cause of blocked airways.

Once the airways are clear, check that the hawk is breathing. Very often, once the airways are clear, the hawk will recommence breathing without any help. If the hawk does not start breathing once the airways are cleared, then you must take immediate action, otherwise the hawk will die. Artificial respiration, though difficult, is possible with hawks. If a hawk has stopped breathing, rather than give mouth-to-mouth respiration, hold the hawk by its legs and, keeping your arms straight, swing the hawk to left and then to right. This transfers the weight of the hawk's internal organs on and off the diaphragm, causing the lungs to fill and empty of air. Keep this up until the hawk begins breathing on its own, until help arrives, or until you believe the hawk is beyond help.

When the hawk is breathing you should concern yourself with the heart and/or bleeding. If the hawk is not conscious, you should check that the hawk's heart is beating. This is best achieved by placing your ear against its chest and listening intently. An animal as small as a hawk has only a small heart, and consequently the heart sounds will be very difficult to hear. A stethoscope is an obvious advantage here but it is unlikely that, in a first aid situation, one will always be to hand. An indication of the hawk's heart beat is the colour of the mucous membranes inside the hawk's mouth. If the hawk's heart is beating normally, then its blood circulation will be normal and the gums should be pink. If the gums are pale or white, this could indicate a serious circulation problem, such as internal bleeding, heart failure or shock. If, on the other hand, the gums are bright red, this could indicate toxaemia (an overwhelming systemic infection) – a potentially serious condition.

If you are certain that the hawk's heart has stopped, lay the hawk on its left hand side and apply *gentle* pressure to its rib cage. You will feel the rib cage move about 10 to 20 mm (½ to 1 inch), dependent on species. Do not push. Release the pressure. This is one cycle. Repeat a cycle about every couple of seconds.

Once the hawk is breathing, if it does not return to consciousness, ensure that you keep a check on its breathing whilst checking for other injuries.

If the hawk is unconscious and bleeding from its ears, nose or mouth, try to keep the hawk horizontal and immobilised, and do not move the hawk more than you have to. Such symptoms could indicate cervical (neck) injuries, which often occur at the same time as injuries to the head. If the hawk is suffering such injuries, too much movement may result in permanent injury or paralysis.

While attending the hawk, take note of its breathing; is it fast or slow? Smooth and easy or laboured? Check the pupils – are they dilated or very small? Are the hawk's muscles supple or stiff? Is the hawk responsive to voices and/or touch? All such information will help the veterinary surgeon treat the hawk's injuries, and could save its life.

Remember to ensure your own safety at all times.

FIRST AID KIT

A well-stocked first aid kit is essential for both hawks and humans when out on a hawking venture, and also at base. Some of the most common hawk injuries – minor cuts and abrasions – occur when the hawk is being worked, and it is important that these injuries are treated as soon as possible to minimise any adverse effects on the hawk. In order to do this, a small first aid kit should be kept in the building housing the hawks, and a first aid kit should also be taken along on every hawking foray. Of course, you must have the necessary skill and experience to treat these minor injuries, and it is recommended that the falconer attend a basic first aid course. Where there is any doubt as to the seriousness of a hawk's injuries, or its general condition, veterinary treatment should be sought as soon as is practical.

A suitable first aid kit for both humans and hawks should contain the following items as a minimum, and should always accompany you on any field trip, and be near at hand at all times.

Nail clippers
These should be top quality, and can be used for trimming the hawk's talons. Only use the clippers which work on the guillotine principle, i.e. where one blade hits the other, rather than on the scissors principle. The latter type can result in talons being pulled out.

Tweezers
For the removal of foreign bodies, stings, etc.

Scissors
These should be curved and round-ended, and are to be used to cut away any feathers around a wound – these scissors must *not* be used for trimming a hawk's talons.

Antiseptic lotion
For cleansing cuts, wounds and abrasions. Lotions for humans are just as effective on hawks and can be obtained from any pharmacy.

Antiseptic wound powder
This should be applied to wounds after they have been thoroughly cleansed, when it will serve to dry the wound, cleanse it and prevent ingress of dirt, etc., as well as aiding the healing process.

Antiseptic ointment
This ointment can be used instead of, or in conjunction with, antiseptic powder. We use an ointment that is coloured a vivid green, which helps to indicate to everyone exactly where the hawk's wound is.

Cotton wool
Used for cleaning wounds, cuts and abrasions, and for stemming the flow of blood. Ensure it is kept in airtight containers to prevent soiling.

Surgical gauze
Used for padding wounds and stemming the flow of blood. This is supplied in sterile packaging. Once opened, any surplus gauze must be disposed of, and must never be used for wound dressing, etc., as it will no longer be sterile.

Adhesive plasters
Although these will soon be pulled and bitten off by the hawk, they are useful for applying directly to small wounds and for keeping dressings in place, and can also be used for minor splinting. Keep a range of sizes, remembering that large plasters can be cut to size, whereas small ones cannot be enlarged.

Bandages
A selection of small bandages should be kept for binding broken limbs and wounds. They will, of course, be temporary, as the hawk will bite or pull them off. Again, a selection of suitable sizes should be kept in the first aid box.

Cotton buds
Ideal for cleaning wounds and for the application of ointments, etc.

Table salt
A solution of table salt – two teaspoons of salt to 0.5 litres (1 pint) of water – is a good solution to wash debris from wounds and to counter infection. When applying such a solution, it can be drizzled/poured onto the wound to wash out debris; it is also excellent for washing out eyes. Take care that the contaminated solution does not flow into other wounds or into healthy eyes.

Sodium bicarbonate
On a wet compress, this will help reduce swelling.

Styptic pencil
Sold in pharmacies and made from aluminium sulphate, one of these will help to stem the flow of blood from wounds. Be aware, however, that styptic pencils sting on application to an open wound, and the hawk may well react aggressively to the application of this material.

Haemorrhoid ointment
Extremely useful for treating soft tissue bruising.

Stethoscope
To check for the hawk's heart beat. These instruments need not be particularly expensive, but users need some basic training in their use. Ask your vet to show you how to use one and how to identify the different sounds heard through this instrument. It can also be used to listen to the sound of lungs, the stomach and other parts of the hawk's internal workings.

Hypodermic syringes
These are essential for administering liquid medication orally. Keep a range of sizes in the kit.

Many of the items listed can be used on both hawk and human injuries, and most are available from pharmacies and pet shops. Specialised items can be obtained from veterinary practices.

Where items of equipment are involved, it is vital that the user has experience of these items *before* they are needed in an emergency situation. At times of emergency, stress levels of all concerned are high, and having to work out how to use a piece of equipment will do nothing to reduce these levels. Similarly, such 'simple' procedures as bandaging should be practised before they are needed to be used on a sick or injured hawk.

RECOGNISING SICKNESS IN A HAWK

HEALTH

Very often, the falconer will notice 'something not quite right' with his hawk, without really being able to put his finger on just what exactly the problem is. It is this 'sixth sense' which often helps get a sick hawk to the vet in time to save its life.

More obvious signs of sickness in a hawk are changes in its behaviour, body functions or demeanour. A fit hawk will sit on the fist, not bate (provided it has been properly manned), happily and enthusiastically chase its quarry or the lure, and eat its feed with great exuberance and even impatience. When resting, such a hawk will sit with feathers fluffed up, one leg raised, and its wings crossed over the top of its train (tail) (longwings only).

A hawk in low condition will not fly very strongly and will tire easily, often leading to it giving up the chase on the quarry or pitching (landing) when flown to the lure. Such a hawk will grab at its food and take one or two quick bites, but then stand holding it without eating, for some time. When it sits on its block, it may sit on both feet, or on one foot and the knuckle of the other, and its wings may well droop below its train. If it has the strength to bate, such bating will be obviously weak.

If a hawk is seen to be on its block, standing on both feet, feathers fluffed and eyes half-closed, and generally seems uncoordinated, it is in a very low condition, and extremely close to death.

Loss of weight, loss of appetite, half-closed eyes, reluctance to move, a change in the appearance of its mutes and/or casts, and vomiting are all signs of a sick hawk which needs to be taken to a veterinary surgeon without delay. Likewise, a hawk having trouble breathing or suffering from twitching, fits or convulsions will need the urgent attentions of a veterinary surgeon.

When a sick hawk is found, it should be handled as little as possible, since handling will increase its stress levels and this may aggravate the hawk's medical condition; instead, the sick hawk should be placed in its darkened carry box, which is then placed near to a gentle heat source, such as a central heating radiator.

Sick hawks dehydrate rapidly, and will require the administration of rehydrating fluids. This procedure is fairly simple, but it is best if the falconer is shown how to carry out the procedure by an experienced practitioner or veterinary surgeon before attempting it himself.

To give rehydrating fluid by mouth will require a crop tube, a 120 to 150-mm (5 to 6-inch) length of soft plastic or rubber tubing attached to a syringe. With an assistant firmly but gently restraining and holding the sick hawk's head, while at the same time straightening the hawk's neck, the falconer will insert the tube into the hawk's mouth, and then down past the side of the opening of the windpipe, into its crop. The windpipe is easily recognised and avoided, as it appears as a slit in the hawk's tongue.

Rehydrating fluids are readily available from veterinary surgeries and pet shops. However, if a dehydrated hawk is found and the falconer has no such fluid, an effective substitute can be made as follows:

Mix together
- ½ litre (1 pint) warm water
- 1 tablespoon sugar (Where it is available, glucose is better than household sugar, as it is more easily assimilated by the affected hawk)
- 1 teaspoon salt

BLAIN

See 'Carpal bursitis' below.

BUMBLEFOOT

This is the generic term given to inflamed and infected feet of hawks, and is caused by infection or injury. Poorly designed and maintained perches are a classic cause of this affliction in hawks. Veterinary treatment must be sought.

CARPAL BURSITIS

Commonly referred to as 'blain' by falconers, this disease appears after some trauma and takes the form of a soft, fluid-filled swelling on the hawk's wrist or elbow joint. Such swellings almost inevitably result in severe arthritis in the hawk's joints, preventing the hawk from flying. In all such cases, veterinary treatment must be sought.

COLDS AND CHILLS

If it is suspected that a hawk may have breathing problems, loss of appetite and/or weight, and a general lack of condition, a mute sample should be taken for pathological examination. From the results of this examination, a veterinary surgeon will probably prescribe a course of antibiotics for the ailing hawk.

DRY GANGRENE SYNDROME

See 'Wing-tip oedema'.

FEATHER DISORDERS

Most feather problems are the result of parasitic infection, although feathers may also be damaged by trauma, and deficiencies in a hawk's diet may result in poor feathers. Veterinary examination will usually reveal the cause, enabling the vet to prescribe the correct treatment for the hawk.

FROSTBITE

See 'Wing-tip Oedema'.

HYPOCALCAEMIA

A lack of calcium can cause a hawk to fit and this condition is most evident in poorly nourished young hawks, egg-laying females, and stressed accipiters. Veterinary treatment is essential. This will consist of the administration of calcium borogluconate and dietary supplementation with vitamin D.

HYPOGLYCAEMIA

Small hawks, especially muskets (male sparrowhawks) are particularly prone to this affliction, which is caused by extremely low levels of blood glucose. Treatment, which may be administered by the falconer, consists of the oral administration of glucose solution via a crop tube.

LEAD POISONING

Where a hawk is seen to be behaving in a particularly 'nervous' manner, lead poisoning should be suspected. Examples are when the hawk seems listless, weak and has drooping wings. As the condition worsens, the hawk will sit back on its hocks and its feet, turned inwards, will be permanently clasped. The lead poisoning could be the result of ingestion of lead shot in feed, or the hawk itself may have suffered gunshot wounds. An X-ray examination will need to be undertaken to find the offending lead, which will then require surgical removal by a veterinary surgeon.

PARASITES

Internal or endo-parasites

All hawks can suffer from internal parasites such as worms and fluke. Diagnosis is via mute examination, which should be carried out every six months on all of a falconer's hawks. Treatment is straightforward, once the specific endo-parsite has been positively identified.

External or ecto-parasites

Excessive preening or feather-pulling in a hawk may well be a sign of ecto-parasite infection. While some of these are visible to the naked eye, others are not, and some even live within the feather itself. In all cases of suspected ecto-parasite infestation, the hawk should be examined by a veterinary surgeon who, once he has positively identified the offending wee beastie, will be able to prescribe the correct treatment.

SINUSITIS

A nasal discharge, a swelling under the eye, or a weeping discharge from the eye may be symptoms of sinusitis. Veterinary examination is necessary in order for the correct treatment to be initiated.

SOUR CROP

Where a hawk does not empty its crop (gorge) for several hours, it is vital that the crop is emptied, otherwise the contents will 'go off', and the toxins thus produced will quickly pass into the hawk's bloodstream resulting in the death of the hawk. Where the offending food is dry e.g. pieces of meat, it is quite easy to simply massage the crop in an upwards motion to bring the food to the hawk's mouth, from where it can be removed via fingers or tweezers. This procedure must not, however, be carried out where the contents of the crop are liquid, as it then becomes all too easy for this liquid to be inhaled, leading to the death of the hawk. In such cases, the services of a veterinary surgeon are required; the vet will administer anaesthetics to the hawk, before passing an inflated tube down the hawk's windpipe while the crop is emptied. The inflated tube will prevent inhalation of any fluids.

STOMATITIS

Known to generations of falconers as 'frounce', stomatitis is caused by *Trichomonas gallinae*, a protozoan parasite. Hawks infected with this will have a reduced appetite and will be generally lethargic. Usually, the inside of the affected hawk's mouth is coated with a white lesion, resembling plaque. Once positively identified by a veterinary surgeon, treatment with an antiprotozoal drug is simple and effective.

THIAMINE DEFICIENCY

A member of the B vitamin group, a deficiency of this vitamin can cause fits in hawks. A full veterinary examination, including the blood, will have to be undertaken to confirm this diagnosis. Once this has been confirmed, the hawk can usually be maintained on a diet high in thiamine.

TRAUMA

Bite wounds

Usually on the hawk's legs and feet, these wounds need to be treated as soon as possible after the injury. Clean the wound and cover with antiseptic ointment or powder. If the wound bleeds profusely, apply pressure to stem the flow of blood. Where the limb swells for more than eight hours, a veterinary surgeon is likely to prescribe a course of antibiotics.

Broken toes

Usually caused when the hawk strikes its prey, broken toes should be treated by a veterinary surgeon, who will need to ensure the alignment of the two broken ends of the bone.

WING-TIP OEDEMA

Sometimes referred to as 'Dry Gangrene Syndrome', caused by keeping tethered hawks close to the floor, with no, or insufficient, heating. Severe cases will lead to the amputation of part of the hawk's wing(s) and thus the end of its flying career.

CHAPTER 10
CAPTIVE BREEDING

During the late 1960s and early 1970s, conservationists realised that the wild population of raptors was in decline, almost worldwide. While there were many reasons for this, the main culprit was the chemical DDT (dichloro diphenyl trichloroethane), an organochloride insecticide widely used in the years after the Second World War. The use of this chemical led to the devastation of populations of predatory raptors, as it caused the shells of the birds' eggs to be so thin that, when the female sat on the eggs for incubation, the eggs cracked and broke.

In the USA, a group of conservation scientists, falconers and other interested parties formed the Peregrine Fund, and began a captive breeding programme for the peregrine falcon (*Falco peregrinus*), and it is the work of this dedicated band that inspired others throughout the world to begin other raptor propagation programmes. Today, one of the main methods used in captive breeding by falconers is one which owes all to the Peregrine Fund – artificial insemination (AI). Used by the Peregrine Fund scientists to propagate more pure peregrines, many falconers today use the technique to produce hybrid hawks, as well as pure bred

Inside the author's incubation room. A selection of raptor eggs in the foreground, with two small incubators behind.

hawks. The Peregrine Fund's breeding programme was so successful that they bred and released over three thousand peregrines in North America, a testimony to the hard work and professionalism of all involved with the project.

Although our predecessors would have taken their hawks from the wild population, in the modern world this is no longer acceptable, and so falconers must work to produce self-sustaining populations of raptors from which falconers can take hawks for sporting use. In addition, the skills learned and knowledge amassed through such endeavours can be put to use for pure conservation purposes.

Before beginning a captive breeding programme, the falconer needs to look carefully at the resources he has, those he will need, and the possible end results of his labours. In general, the success achieved in a breeding programme will be directly proportional to the amount of work, time and effort that the falconer puts into the project. If the main driving force for the breeding programme is to make large amounts of money, a rethink is needed. Today, mainly due to captive breeding, the price of raptors is low, and seems to be dropping even lower every year. About twenty years ago, a Harris' hawk would have cost the equivalent of a man's yearly salary, while today, these hawks are often sold at less than a week's wages. While it is true that some species of raptors are holding their prices, and some are even increasing in value, some species are no longer bred by many falconers as the cost of producing these birds is greater than the price one can ask for them on the open market.

PLANNING

The first decision that must be taken by the aspiring raptor breeder is that of species to be bred. With so many different species of raptor available the choice can be daunting, but the novice is recommended to begin with one or more of the more straightforward species to breed in captivity, such as the Harris' hawk, the lanner falcon and the saker falcon. Once this decision has been taken, the breeder should look at housing requirements and build aviaries which are suitable for the intended species.

HOUSING

Most raptor breeders favour seclusion aviaries when they will be using naturally paired raptors, rather than AI. These aviaries have solid sides, in order that the passage of humans does not disturb the hawks; a top which is only partly covered with solid sheets of metal or timber; and the rest of the roof is made of strong, welded wire mesh.

The aviary should be as large as possible, and give the inmates the opportunity to carry out their natural behaviour. On average, 6 x 4 x 3 m (19 x 13 x 10 feet) high is a good size for a breeding aviary. It should have footings of concrete blocks, with a concrete floor built to slope slightly towards a drainage area. The timber used should be external quality (or marine) plywood, securely fastened on to a timber frame of 50 x 50 mm (2 x 2 inch) uprights and cross-pieces. The roof should have one third covered by plastic or metal sheeting, with strong weld wire mesh over the rest. *Never use 'chicken mesh'*, as this is wire that is simply twisted together, is not very strong and can easily become untwisted, allowing the hawks to escape or predators to get into the aviary.

The concrete floor of the aviary can be covered by small gravel chips (pea gravel), and the timber should be treated with animal-friendly paint or timber treatment. A nest ledge will be needed for most species, although some hawks and owls prefer to nest on the ground. Several perches will be necessary, and these should be of different thicknesses and set at different heights – at least one perch should be set at a height which will easily accommodate a copulating pair of raptors (for most species one metre/39 inches is sufficient head room). We like to put a couple of perches under the shelter of the solid roof and a couple under the welded mesh area. The nest ledge should always be under cover.

Four lanner (*Falco biarmicus*) eggs in an incubator at The National Falconry School. Note the temperature has dropped due to the open door.

On the nest ledge, the breeder will need to supply suitable nesting material. For falcons, we use a square box-like structure, measuring about one metre (39 inches) square, with a height of approximately 100 mm (4 inches) filled with pea gravel. For our Harris' hawks, we affix a triangular piece of strong timber across a corner of the aviary. We take a car tyre, bind it together to close up the central gap, and fasten the tyre to the shelf. Inside the tyre, we put several handfuls of wood shavings, and some small branches.

Over all nest ledges in all of our breeding aviaries, we position a small CCTV camera, capable of producing images even in the depths of night and we have another CCTV camera in each aviary covering the other parts of the enclosure. These cameras are wired to a screen positioned in the School's office, from where the activities of each aviary can be monitored.

All hawks need to bathe and drink, especially egg-laying females, and so a bath should be built into the design. The bath needs to be positioned so that the hawks are unlikely to mute (defecate) into it, and the humans servicing the aviary easily reach it. Many breeders set up a type of drawer system for the baths, allowing them to be cleaned and refilled without too much disturbance to the hawks.

SELECTING BREEDING STOCK

Once the breeder has decided on the species to be bred, he must next consider the methods to be used. Will the raptors be natural pairs? Or will the breeder be utilising AI methods? Will the breeder wish to acquire adult hawks or youngsters which will not breed for several seasons?

If it is wished to use AI, then the hawks needed for the breeding programme will need to be imprinted.

IMPRINTED HAWKS

All imprinted hawks or imprints, are raised by the human hand, to a greater or lesser degree, and with some subtle – but important – differences. The methods used to imprint a hawk will have a profound effect on it and its behaviour towards humans and other hawks.

A sociable imprint is one which is reared by the human hand either from the day it hatches (especially if artificially incubated) or taken from the nest between ten and fourteen days of age. Kept in a warm cage (a brooder) until it can be safely kept in an open-topped enclosure at ambient temperature, the young hawk is kept where it sees people at all times (the breeder usually keeps the young hawk in the human home). Here at the National Falconry School, we raise such imprints in our office, where they see a constant stream of people coming and going. At a very early age, the young hawk is taught to take feed from a dish, and this dish is kept constantly full so that the hawk will never go hungry. This will ensure that the hawk does not feel the need to call to the falconer for food. As it matures, the young hawk will get stronger and more curious, and start climbing out of its enclosure and walking to you. At this stage in its life, the young hawk is referred to as a 'brancher', and it will often climb onto the breeder's lap, where it will lie and sleep.

Trips out and about are the order of the day for the young hawk once it has reached brancher stage, as the hawk will then get a view of the larger picture of the world. On warm days, the youngster can be put on the lawn, as long as it is watched over by its human keeper. We often take the youngsters out on the picnic area, while we have our lunch, sitting the hawk on a spare table or a nearby wall. Feeding at this stage is still *ad liberatum*. As the hawk matures it will readily accept you, and become a pleasure to train and fly.

For AI breeding purposes, a hawk will need to be a 'dual imprint'. For this, an imprinted female (as detailed above) will raise the young while, at the same time, allowing the breeder to openly come and go in the aviary where she is kept. As she is imprinted, she will have no worries about the presence of the human(s) while going about her normal business of rearing young. Hawks raised in this way will accept both hawks and humans, seeing them both as equals. When sexually mature, both males and females will be able to mate with other hawks, but will also wish to copulate with humans, thereby making them ideal for AI purposes.

We prefer to have our breeding stock from youngsters, rather than buy them at breeding age. We will fly them for falconry purposes and will try to fly a potential breeding pair as a cast. In this way, the relationship between the two hawks develops, and we have found that we get a very high rate of success with such couples.

ARTIFICIAL INCUBATION

Not all animals make good parents and it is a wise breeder who remembers this truth. We have had some of our hawks who clumsily knock eggs from the nest ledges, while others stamp on the eggs, breaking or cracking them; some hawks will kill and eat their young. Such hawks can either be taken out of the breeding programme or their eggs can be collected and artificially incubated. When we take eggs, we take them as they are laid, although some breeders will wait for the female to sit the full clutch of eggs for seven to ten days before removing them. Some breeders use broody bantam hens (chickens) to incubate the hawk eggs naturally for the first week or so, but many simply place the eggs in a top-class incubator from day one.

Any incubator used for raptor eggs will need to be a first-rate machine, capable of maintaining an even, set temperature at all times. The incubator should also have automatic turning facilities and, ideally, a humidity control. Size is not important for such a machine, as relatively small numbers of eggs will be incubated at any one time. It is preferable to have several small incubators, rather than one huge incubator, to keep to the adage that one should not put all one's eggs in one basket. There are

Another incubator at The National Falconry School. Note the industrial mincer in the background; this is used to mince complete rats, quail, mice, etc. for feeding to young hawks. Note also the temperature; the incubator is warming up.

many good incubators on the market, and time and effort should be devoted to researching the best for any particular breeding programme.

As artificial incubators are dependent on the electricity supply, the breeder should take steps to deal with any interruption to that supply. At the very least, an alarm should be used which will signal to the breeder if the electricity supply fails so the breeder can make alternative arrangements for the incubator. At the other end of the spectrum, and essential if large numbers of expensive and/or rare raptor eggs are to be incubated, a breeder may have his own back-up generator which will automatically and seamlessly kick in in the event of a failure of the mains electricity supply.

The optimum temperature for incubating raptor eggs is 37.5 °C (99.5 °F), and an accurate thermometer is another essential piece of equipment which must be purchased. Most suppliers of incubation equipment will sell a wide range of thermometers, and the breeder should buy the best he can afford – this will be a first-class thermometer which has been calibrated in a specialist laboratory.

We have set aside a specific room as our incubation room. The room is well insulated to help minimise fluctuations in temperature, which would obviously have an effect on the efficiency of the incubators used. The room has no windows, and its own thermostatically controlled heating system. In addition it is fitted with a dehumidifier, an item of equipment we find is essential in England in order to keep the raptor eggs at the correct humidity level. Staff using the incubation room have to walk though a disinfectant foot bath, and wear clean white coats, which are kept in the room and cannot be taken out other than to be laundered.

Before using any incubator, brooder or similar item of equipment, we ensure that it has been thoroughly cleaned with a suitable disinfectant, and then we 'gas' the machines. To do this, we place the incubator etc. in a small room kept for the purpose. Next we place a small dish in the bottom of the incubator, which is running at the correct temperature, and add 0.4 g of potassium permanganate. Wearing protective gloves and a mask, the technician next adds 0.8 ml of formaldehyde to the potassium permanganate. This starts a reaction which produces a mild gas which has a disinfecting action. The gas formed is also a mild tear gas and so our technicians wear a suitable mask to protect themselves from this while 'gassing out' the incubators, brooders, etc.

On average, it takes between thirty-one and thirty-two days for an egg to reach

A selection of hawk eggs (lanner and ferruginous) about to be candled to test for fertility.

'pip' when the chick will start breaking out of the egg. During this time, the egg will constantly lose water through its shell, and this will cause the egg to lose weight. If the egg loses too much water, the chick will desiccate (dry up) and die; if the egg does not lose enough water, the chick will drown. On collection of the eggs, they are weighed on an extremely accurate set of scales, with the weight being taken to

The egg of a ferruginous buzzard (*Buteo regalis*), being weighed prior to incubation. Note the digital callipers, used to measure the eggs.

0.1 grams, and this weight is recorded. If all goes according to plan, and the eggs are incubated at the correct temperature and humidity, each egg will lose about 15% of its weight during incubation (about half a per cent per day), and we draw a graph for each egg which predicts the weight of that egg on any one day. The graph is checked every twenty four hours, in order for us to be able to monitor the weight loss, and make any adjustments to the incubation that we feel are necessary.

We start incubating every egg in a dry incubator, i.e. one without water in it, and which will then operate at ambient humidity. If an egg is losing too much weight (i.e. too much water is evaporating through the shell), we either move the egg to an incubator with higher humidity, or paint thin strips of nail varnish on the egg shell, to prevent it from losing so much water. Conversely, if the egg is not losing enough weight (i.e. not enough water is evaporating through its shell), we will place the egg in a 'dry' incubator into which we place silica gel, which readily absorbs water in the atmosphere. This silica gel will require changing every twenty four hours, if it is to keep the incubator 'dry'.

The incubators we use have an automatic turning mechanism, and ours are set to keep the egg turning – very slowly and very gently – almost continuously. On the day of pip, the egg must not be turned any more, since this will disorientate the chick inside. We remove the egg from the incubator and place this in a 'brooder'.

Some breeders use rather hit or miss brooders, which can easily undo the work of the incubator. We refuse to do this, and have invested in several 'Animal Intensive Care Units' (AICU) manufactured by Lyons Electrical Company. This is a very expensive and sophisticated piece of equipment that was designed, veterinary tested and proven by Hannis L. Stoddard III, DVM. The AICU is manufactured from acrylic

Animal Intensive Care Unit (AICU).

which is lightweight and extremely durable. The heating console contains solid state electronics with an electrostatic filtering system, and is easily removed to allow the main plastic case to be submerged for total cleaning and disinfection. The humidity within the AICU is maintained by adjustable vents and a water tray, and the internal temperature of the unit can be maintained between ambient and 37.7 °C (100 °F). This piece of equipment is a good investment for any professionally minded raptor breeder, and will soon repay the investment.

We set the AICU's temperature to 37.7 °C (100 °F), and fill the AICU's water reservoir, which raises the humidity within the unit. This is vital, since low humidity will cause the chick to stick to the egg shell, and could easily lead to the death of the baby hawk. The egg is placed in a small plastic tub; we use small sandwich boxes, measuring about 130 x 80 x 60 mm (5 x 3 x 2½ inches), although many breeders use empty margarine containers. Whichever container is used, it must be scrupulously clean, and we physically wash ours and then put them through a dishwasher, which works on extremely high temperature steam cleaning principles. In the bottom of the container, we place a folded piece of kitchen roll, tissue, paper towel or similar.

A chick can take up to forty-eight or more hours to hatch, but the vast majority emerge from their shells within twenty four to thirty six hours of pip. At this stage, the chick will be very wet, and we leave it in its container, in the AICU, until it is thoroughly dried, at which stage the chick is transferred to another clean sandwich box container, with clean tissue in the bottom, and then placed in another AICU. Here the temperature is set at 36.5 °C (98 °F), and the humidity is ambient, i.e. the water reservoir in the AICU is empty. We mark each chick, using a permanent felt marker, with its own unique reference number; these marks are made on the back of the chick, but we also place a small piece of plastic (about 30 x 30 mm / 1¼ x 1¼ inches) in the bottom of the sandwich box, and write the same reference on that. As the chick is cleaned out (after every feeding), this reference card is also cleaned and replaced in the fresh box.

Temperature control, correct nutrition and hygiene are all essential elements to the successful rearing of young hawks. The temperature will need to be slowly reduced; the actual temperature will depend upon species, and varies considerably. A good indicator of the comfort of the chick is that those feeling too warm will lie flattened on the base of their container; those too cold will sit huddled up. In the former case, the chick is likely to be panting, while in the latter, it will be shivering. If you are breeding large numbers of hawks, it is worth investing in several AICUs. This will enable you to run them at different temperatures, and move the chicks as required, rather than trying to adjust each AICU constantly.

FEEDING YOUNG HAWKS

A 5-day old Harris' hawk, still in the incubation facilities. Note the small plastic box which is the ideal size to hold a young hawk. The box is lined with tissue paper, which makes the box easy to clean and gives the hawk's feet something on which to grip, thus preventing splayed legs.

We never feed a chick until twelve hours after its hatch. During this time, the chick will obtain sustenance from its egg sac, which is absorbed into the stomach on the day of pip. The first meal we give the youngsters is one of quail breast meat, and we only give a very small amount. The food is freshly prepared, and the chick is fed using sterilised forceps. We always dip each piece of food into warm water as we are feeding it to the hawk as this water lubricates the feed, warms it and at the same time gives the youngster fluid.

Young longwings will require a 'chup' noise to get their attention for feeding, but both shortwings and broadwings react to the sight of the food in the forceps.

We weigh each chick before and after feeding, and record this information. On the first few feeds, as we gently tap the hawk's beak with the forceps (loaded with a small piece of meat), the young hawk will valiantly try to grab at the meat, but will be too uncoordinated to do so. To help it, we gently hold its head in the circle formed by a finger and thumb. Within a few days, the hawk has got the hang of this, and support is no longer required. Each meal will get slightly bigger, but we never force the hawk to eat more than it wants. Experienced breeders will tell you that more young hawks are killed by overfeeding than by underfeeding. We normally feed three times each day – early morning, mid afternoon, and evening – leaving the birds in peace during the night time. If we return to the hawk and find that it still has food in its crop, we leave it for another hour before trying again.

We keep feeding quail breast meat until the third day, when we feed freshly killed and minced carcasses – we tend to favour rat pups or young mice for this. We also mix in small amounts of vitamin and mineral supplements, the amount and timing of which varies according to the supplement used, and so the breeder should read the manufacturer's instructions on this matter.

At about seven days, unless the hawk is to be imprinted, we put the young hawks with their parents. Another alternative is to raise many young hawks together; this is known as crèche rearing or cohort rearing. If attempting crèche rearing, the breeder is recommended to rear longwings together, broadwings together and shortwings together, but not to mix the groups. Shortwings, in particular, are extremely aggressive towards their siblings, and the weaker and/or more timid individuals will not be able to feed sufficiently.

RINGING

In the UK, by law, all raptors indigenous to the European Union (EU) will need to be fitted with a closed ring, on which is inscribed a unique number. While some breeders will have their own details put on these rings, it is best to use those issued by a nationally recognised body, such as the Independent Bird Register (IBR – see Appendix 3).

Hawks included under Schedule 4 of the Wildlife & Countryside Act, must be fitted

An example of the versatility of the Harris' hawk. This male hawk was trained to fly over central London, carrying a small video camera, and film the area for an arts project.

with a suitable ring issued by Defra, and all hawks and owls which are classed as being indigenous to the EU must also have an Article 10 (A10), if they are to be sold, used for breeding, displayed for commercial purposes or offered for sale.

Each species will require a different size ring, and females of that species a larger ring than the males. Full details of these sizes can be obtained from the IBR, Defra and similar organisations.

RECORDS

It is in the interests of all concerned for the breeder to keep full and accurate records of all his birds. These will also be required for the granting of Article 10s and other licences necessary to fulfil legal requirements.

CHAPTER 11
LOST BIRDS

Although some falconers will claim never to have lost a hawk, this claim should be taken with a large pinch of salt. There will always be times when, for whatever reason, the hawk simply will not answer the recall whistle or shout. With longwings, it is extremely easy for them to hit a thermal current, which will take them high and far away. Broadwings that learn to soar can also hit a thermal, which may carry them to the far side of a cliff, ridge or mountain. Both shortwings and broadwings flown in wooded areas can become unsighted from the falconer. In all such cases, the hawk is classed as lost, even though the vast majority of these hawks will be safely recovered.

When a hawk is lost, i.e. out of view of the falconer and does not respond to the recall signal, it is important for the falconer to keep cool. Stress levels will rise quickly, and it is all too easy to allow a certain amount of pessimism, gloom and even panic to set in. As stated earlier in this book, I believe that all hawks should be flown with telemetry at all times, and that the falconer should have a good working knowledge of the system used. Always check the system is working *before* allowing the hawk free flight. I am amazed and saddened when I hear so many stories of falconers who did not do this, and the result is almost always a hawk which is not recovered. On one memorable occasion, I was called to a house in Derbyshire, where the occupier had reported a large white bird sitting on the garden shed. When I got there, I recognised the hawk as a female gyr falcon. It responded almost instantaneously to my swung lure, and I soon had it tethered on my fist, while it ate its breakfast. Attached to its train was a telemetry transmitter which I removed for safety. I opened the transmitter to remove the batteries, only to discover that the battery chamber was empty. When the hawk was safely returned to its rightful owner, I questioned the lack of batteries, and the falconer replied that he had simply forgotten to put them in the transmitter. Had he checked before releasing his hawk, he could have made the recovery himself. He was extremely lucky that the hawk had decided to land in the garden of someone who knew to report the event.

When a hawk is lost, head for the highest piece of ground, from where you should be able to see the area where the hawk was last spotted. Using the telemetry, check for a signal. It is also useful to call the hawk and use the swing lure, as these actions may well grab its attention and bring it back to the falconer without any further drama.

Lost hawks tend to fly downwind, and so if there is no signal or visual sighting of the hawk, the falconer should head in that direction. If a vehicle is used, more ground can be covered more quickly, but the vehicle must make frequent stops to check for any signal on the telemetry. Vehicles can be fitted with an aerial which is mounted on the roof, and where a car is used a lot for falconry purposes, this can be a distinct advantage.

Rooks and other birds will often mob a hawk, and the falconer and his assistants should keep looking and listening for any sign of such mobbing, which must be investigated. The more people who can be enlisted to help, the better, provided that they are sensible people. When asking members of the public if they have seen your lost hawk, their responses must be treated with the utmost caution. On more than one occasion I have been told that a hawk is sitting in a particular tree, only to discover that it is a woodpigeon.

If the hawk is not recovered within a few hours, the falconer must report his lost hawk to the IBR, the police and the RSPCA. Do not expect any of these organisations to launch a massive hawk-hunt; they will simply respond to any reports that they may receive regarding a strange bird, and then get back to you. Ensure that you have a working mobile phone and that the authorities are given that number.

To aid recovery of the hawk, it should be fitted, ideally, with a closed ring giving a contact telephone number, which of course must be manned throughout the period that the hawk is missing.

If a hawk is found at night, it can be quite difficult to effect recovery, especially if it is sitting high in a tree, on a cliff ledge or atop a large building. To facilitate such recoveries, we train all of our hawks to respond to the lure when it is illuminated, in exactly the same way that we train the hawks for lamping, and we periodically practice this with each hawk.

If a closed ring with a telephone number is not on the hawk, attach a small disk, such as those sold by pet shops for cats and small dogs, to an aylmeri. In the past, we have also used small canisters which contain a piece of paper on which can be written your name and contact details. These canisters are still sold in pet shops and veterinary practices for use with dogs and cats.

Any such attachments must be made in such a way that they will not present any danger to the hawk, such as becoming tangled in foliage, etc.

FERRETING CODE OF PRACTICE

INTRODUCTION

Properly conducted, ferreting – the use of ferrets to bolt rabbits from their warrens – is both a sport and one of the most effective methods of controlling the wild rabbit population. It causes little disturbance to the environment and results in healthy fresh meat for the table, and income for local people. Ferreting was the way in which many of us were introduced to the delights of country sports, and its importance to farmers, landowners and country sports enthusiasts should not be underestimated.

However, as with all pastimes – and particularly those involving country sports – all practitioners have to consider public reaction to their actions and the public face of their practices. It is important, therefore, that we all conduct ourselves in a truly acceptable manner at all times. It is hoped that this code of practice will help enshrine our finest traditions and ensure the highest standards from all who participate in this ancient and fascinating sport. This Code was produced in conjunction and cooperation with the BASC, the Countryside Alliance, and the Game and Wildlife Conservation Trust, formerly known as the Game Conservancy, and is the only such Code to have achieved approval by all of these leading UK country sports organisations.

With the increase in the UK's rabbit population, farmers and landowners are fighting a constant battle against this pest. No one wishes to see the elimination of the rabbit, but the damage that it does to agriculture is colossal. Five rabbits eat as much food as a sheep, and there are currently an estimated 45+ million rabbits in the UK. Most people would agree that it is more sensible, humane and 'environmentally friendly' to control this burgeoning rabbit population by means of ferreting than by using poisons, gassing or by the introduction of diseases specifically intended to destroy the rabbit population *en masse*.

When the UK rabbit population reached epidemic proportions (over 100 million) in the early 1950s, myxomatosis was introduced by humans and the disease killed 99% of the rabbit population of England and Wales within six months. While there can be no argument that this reduced the rabbit population, the pain, distress and suffering that it caused has shocked many a true country person.

Even within the relatively small area of these islands, there are many variations – including climate and crops – which will affect ferreting, but it is the spirit of this Code which is important. All true country sports enthusiasts should encourage its use, support those who adhere to it, and draw it to the attention of all interested parties.

THE RULES

> 1. All ferreting operations must be conducted in strict accord with the laws relating to all aspects of the sport, and it is the duty of all ferreters to understand and observe these laws.

The laws which apply to ferreting are many and varied, including those protecting property, the person and the welfare of animals. All ferreters should understand the reasons for these laws, the importance of observing them and the consequences of breaking them. The old maxim that ignorance is no excuse should be borne in mind at all times.

Ferreting is also a sport and, even where the intention is to control the rabbit population, the best traditions of country sports should be upheld and practised.

> 2. Ferreting must only be carried out with the permission of the landowner or duly authorised tenant over whose land you intend to ferret. Operations should be limited to the areas, times and dates stipulated by that person.

It is a wise precaution to have permission in writing, and this should be carried at all times while out ferreting over that area. It is also common sense to inform the landowner/tenant when you will be working a specific area, and check that this is convenient. Be prepared to avoid any areas if requested, and stick to the letter of your agreement. This is particularly important during the game shooting or hunting seasons.

> 3. As far as possible, ferreting should be limited to times of the year when there are fewest litters of rabbits, normally from September to the middle of March (although this may vary with geographical location of site).

It is in no-one's interests to ferret burrows where many of the does will have litters.

> 4.   At least one member of the ferreting team should have considerable experience of the sport, and all involved should be competent in the humane killing of captured rabbits.

Ferreting can be a complicated exercise and considerable skill, born of experience, is needed to carry out the work efficiently and effectively. Practitioners should acquire those skills and experience under the watchful eye of seasoned ferreters.

All members of the ferreting team should be able to identify signs of badgers, which are highly protected and the deliberate disturbance of which is illegal. No ferreting or disturbance of any kind should be carried out in or near badger setts, even if there are signs of rabbits in the same workings; neither should any ferrets be entered into any workings where it is believed that foxes are living, as this is potentially dangerous to the ferrets.

Any dead rabbits found in suspicious circumstances should be reported to the landowner or tenant, as should any signs of poaching. The National Ferret School issues an information sheet on rabbit calici virus (also known as viral haemorrhagic disease – VHD) in wild rabbits.

> 5.   Whenever possible, ferreting should not be carried out single-handedly.

When digging or working in excavations, there is always a risk – however slight – of a lone ferreter becoming trapped or buried alive. The risks are minimised when ferreters work in teams, while this also leads to more efficient and effective rabbit clearance.

Even where small teams go ferreting, it is advisable to inform a responsible person of the exact location(s) of operations, and give an expected time of return. Where ferreters are unavoidably delayed, every effort should be made to inform this person, in order to avoid the unnecessary involvement of the emergency services.

> 6.   An elementary first aid kit should be carried by every ferreting team, and at least one member of the team should have experience and/or training in elementary first aid procedures.

The first aid kit, which will be suitable for use on both human and ferret injuries, and can easily be carried in the net bag, should contain the following:

• Assortment of bandages

- Cotton wool or gauze
- Sticking plasters
- Antiseptic liquid, ointment or powder
- Tweezers
- Scissors

The basic principles of first aid are to save life, prevent the condition worsening and aid the recovery of the victim, and are applicable to both humans and animals. The order in which injuries should be addressed is summed up by the ABC Rule:

A - An open AIRWAY
B - Adequate BREATHING
C - Sufficient CIRCULATION

Many organisations run courses in human first aid techniques (e.g. St John Ambulance, St Andrew's Ambulance Association and the British Red Cross). It is highly recommended that ferreters attend a first aid course as this could save the life of a member of the team.

7.   Veterinary care should be sought at the earliest possible time for any injured ferret, dog or hawk used in ferreting operations.

Even where first aid has been administered correctly, some injuries will still require veterinary attention. Large wounds will need sutures, while other wounds and bites may require the administering of suitable antibiotics or other prescription-only medicines.

8.   Dogs and hawks used with ferrets must be well trained and accepting of ferrets.

Dogs and hawks, both of which can be and often are used in conjunction with ferrets, have the potential to inflict grave injuries on ferrets, and so they must be extremely well trained and have experience of ferrets, in order to minimise the risks of injury to all parties. When a ferret is attacked, it can defend itself by inflicting painful wounds on the attacker – be it dog or hawk – and even the hand of a human intent on helping the beleaguered ferret.

No dog or hawk should be released (slipped) onto quarry until the rabbit is completely clear of the burrow entrances. This will reduce the risk of ferrets being injured and also of injured rabbits escaping down burrows.

The safety and well-being of dogs and hawks is as important as that of the ferrets, and should be given a high priority.

> 9.   Where the intention is to shoot bolting rabbits, Guns must not shoot until the rabbit is in clear view and well clear of the burrow opening. It is all too easy for ferrets to be accidentally shot by those who ignore this simple, common sense rule.

Many ferrets give hard chase to their quarry and are often very close behind the rabbit. It is bad practice – and extremely dangerous – to shoot without clearly identifying one's target. Injured rabbits, shot close to the entrance to their burrow, may kick themselves down the burrow, rendering it impossible for ferreters to dispatch them humanely.

In the UK, little owls (*Athene noctua*) often live in burrows, and it is not unusual for one to fly away from a rabbit burrow during ferreting operations. It is obvious that this protected raptor should not be shot at.

Guns should be placed in such a way as to avoid any risks of accidents to other Guns, while at the same time giving them every opportunity to shoot bolting rabbits.

> 10. Remove all nets from the burrow after the completion of ferreting operations.

The most commonly used nets for ferreting are purse nets, and these are often made of material which is difficult to see when the net is in position over the opening to a rabbit burrow. Ferreters should count the number of nets placed (not an easy task, especially when several operatives are working at the same time), and ensure that the same number are collected in. By using a rubber band to secure each wound-up net stored in one's net bag, and ensuring that these are put on the nets after they have been used, it is easy to see if there are any nets not yet picked up, i.e. there will be one or more 'spare' rubber bands. It is good practice to check the whole area before leaving or moving on to another burrow.

Nets used for ferreting should be checked and serviced regularly, with any damage being repaired before use.

> 11. Any damage to land or property caused by ferreting activities should be repaired before leaving the area.

It is possible for fences to be damaged slightly, or holes (sometimes substantial) to be dug during a day's ferreting, and it is only honourable and fair to repair all damaged items to their original state, if at all possible. Holes not only look unsightly, but are a potential danger to wildlife, livestock and humans. Unless the landowner or tenant specifically requests otherwise, all ferreted holes should be filled in (back-filled). This action serves three worthwhile purposes: it shows clearly which holes have been ferreted, dissuades rabbits from returning and shows areas in which rabbits have returned.

All ferreters should possess adequate third party liability insurance. We recommend a minimum of £5 million. It is also recommended that ferreters should have suitable personal accident insurance. These types of insurance are offered to all members of the British Association for Shooting & Conservation (BASC), as part of their membership package.

> 12.   No ferret should be worked muzzled or coped.

It is unnecessary and potentially dangerous for a ferret to be worked with either a muzzle or a cope in place. This applies to devices made from string, leather, metal, plastic or any other material. It is only a matter of time before working ferrets meet a rat in the burrow and, if the ferret is fitted with a muzzle, it will have no way of defending itself. A cornered rat will attack such a defenceless ferret, inflicting serious injury or even death.

The barbaric practice of breaking or removing a ferret's teeth is unlawful, immoral and entirely needless. Providing that a ferret is not starved, it is highly unlikely, in the event of an underground kill, to eat the dead rabbit and stay underground to sleep off the meal.

Ferrets used for ferreting do not have to be vicious or nasty; on the contrary, everyone will fare better by using 'quiet' (tame and handleable) ferrets at all times.

> 13.   Wherever possible, every ferret used in rabbiting operations should be equipped with an electronic ferret finder.

The easy availability and efficiency of the modern electronic ferret finder should be utilised to find ferrets which have killed underground, become trapped or for other reasons failed to return to the surface. In order to ensure that this equipment operates properly, it should be serviced regularly, and have new batteries fitted at regular intervals and always after extensive usage. The equipment should be checked before leaving base on a ferreting foray and any equipment not working 100% should not be used, but sent to a qualified person for repair. The end of the collar on which the transponder is fastened, should be secured with electrical insulation tape to help minimise the risks of it snagging on roots, etc. It is also advisable to wrap the casing of the transmitter with insulating tape, as this helps minimise the ingress of water.

Where it is not possible to equip every ferret with a transponder, an 'electronic liner' should be used. This is the modern equivalent of the old-fashioned liner but, instead of an actual line, the ferret is equipped with a transponder. Apart from this modernisation, this ferret's function is exactly the same as a traditional liner, i.e. to bolt out ferrets that have laid-up, and then remain with the dead rabbit until dug out by the ferreter.

Should electronic detectors break down or cease to function correctly, it is useful for ferreters to have the knowledge and skills to use a traditional liner, and we recommend that all ferreters learn these skills in advance of such a situation arising.

> 14. Ferrets which do not leave the burrows or otherwise become 'lost' must not be left.

It is likely that some ferrets, entered into a rabbit burrow during rabbit clearance operations, will not come out of their own accord before it is time for the human operatives to leave the area. Every effort must be made to find these animals. The use of an electronic ferret detector will help in this task, and ferreters must be willing to dig to extricate trapped or lost ferrets. Obviously, suitable grafts, chads or spades should be carried by the ferreting team.

An escaped ferret can cause havoc on a formal game shoot, attacking stocks of pheasants and other game birds, while farmers who keep chickens or water fowl will soon realise why the French gave the ferret its name of *poulet chat* (chicken cat). In the UK under the Animal Welfare Act Act, 2006, it is unlawful to abandon an animal in this way.

Where extensive efforts to find the ferret in the burrow have been unsuccessful, other efforts must be made to recapture the ferrets, and live-catch mink traps are ideal for this purpose. One or two should be taken on every ferreting trip, although they may be left in the vehicle until, and unless, they are needed. Traps should be baited with pieces of rabbit, and placed in close proximity to the area in which the missing ferret was last seen or heard. These traps must be inspected every few hours before dark, at dawn the next day, and at regular intervals until the ferret is found or hope abandoned. The latter should not happen until every possible effort has been made to recapture the ferret.

Landowners and tenants in and around the area of the loss should be notified of any missing ferrets, and given a 24-hour contact number to use should the ferret be seen or captured. Where a third party contacts the ferreters to inform them of the capture of a lost ferret, the ferreters should retrieve the ferret within twenty-four hours. A small reward should also be offered along with your sincere gratitude. This also has a public relations angle, and is well worth the small investment for the goodwill which such a gift engenders.

> 15. No fewer than two ferrets should be taken on any rabbiting trip, and no ferrets should be overworked.

Ferrets, like all animals, will tire during working and are then tempted to find a comfortable place in which to rest. This could easily lead to lost ferrets, and much work on the part of the ferreters. It is far better to use ferrets in teams, and alternate between them, allowing each one regular rest periods. Any ferret which shows obvious signs of fatigue should not be used.

> 16. All ferrets used for rabbiting should be fed and watered before work and if necessary during the day.

It is unnecessary and unwise to work hungry ferrets, since they may be too weak to keep going all day and, being hungry, are always tempted to kill and eat any rabbits that they find. All ferrets used for rabbiting should be fed as normal until the day of the operation. A light meal first thing on the morning of the ferreting trip will ensure that they have enough energy to work, will not be so full that they are lethargic, and will not be tempted to kill and eat any of the rabbits they are hunting. When you take a break for sustenance, allow the ferrets a light snack of rabbit heart or liver. Do not forget to allow ferrets to have access to clean drinking water at regular intervals throughout the day.

> 17. Ferrets should be transported in carrying boxes, and not bags, throughout rabbiting operations.

Strong wooden carrying boxes, with adequate ventilation, are safer and far more comfortable for the ferrets. Bags offer little protection against rain, cold, heat or a size 9 boot. The boxes should be filled with dry straw, the amounts varied according to prevailing weather conditions and temperatures. Carrying boxes containing ferrets should not be left in the sun, and care must be exercised when placing them in the car for transport to or from the ferreting venue. No ferret should be left inside a locked car for more than a few minutes.

All boxes should be equipped with a strong, safe method of securing the opening or lid to prevent the escape of the ferrets, and this should be used whenever a ferret is in the box.

---

18.   When ferreting on railway embankments or the verges of main roads, all ferreters should wear high visibility clothing.

For obvious safety reasons, it is vital that drivers can see anyone who may have strayed onto or near roads and railway tracks, and the high visibility jacket is the ideal way of ensuring high visibility. On minor roads, a simple mesh waistcoat may suffice, but near busy main roads, dual carriageways, motorways and railway tracks, it is recommended that jackets which conform to BS56629, Class A, full Appendix G, are worn by all ferreters. You may feel rather self-conscious wearing such a jacket, but it is common sense to protect yourself in this way.

---

19.   Throughout a day's ferreting, the ferret's welfare must be foremost.

At the end of the day, all ferrets should be fed a top-quality meal of reasonable proportions, dried (if necessary) and checked for injuries. Relevant first aid treatment should be administered if necessary, and then the ferrets should be placed in a safe and secure cage or box, which should then be placed in a safe position in your vehicle, before attending to yourself. If necessary, injured ferrets should be taken to a veterinary surgeon.

Once back at base, the ferrets should be removed from their carrying box, checked again, and when you are certain of their well-being, placed back in their own cub or court, along with a fresh meal.

Dogs and hawks used in conjunction with the ferrets should receive similar treatment and care, again before you tend to your own needs.

---

20.   Ferreting relies on the goodwill of landowners and tenants, as well as the efficient, effective and thoughtful operations of ferreters, and this goodwill must be nurtured.

Ferreters should treat all land and property with respect, and honour all agreements made between themselves and the landowner or tenant over whose land they operate. Guests should not be taken onto ferreting land without the prior express permission of the landowner or tenant. Carried out correctly and with courtesy, ferreting should result in a symbiotic relationship, where ferreter, landowner and tenant benefit from a good working relationship. Good ferreters will be recommended to other landowners and tenants.

SUMMARY

This Code of Practice attempts to give outlines on common-sense ways of ensuring the well-being of all involved in ferreting – both animals and humans. Responsible ferreters will already be adhering to the principles set out in this document, but it is hoped that, as well as guiding newcomers to the sport, 'old-hands' will find this Code a reminder of the importance of conducting oneself in an appropriate manner at all times.

Newcomers are also advised to read books on the subject, and to receive adequate training. The National Ferret School runs courses on ferrets, ferreting and related subjects (including the use of dogs, hawks and ferrets together); the School also produces fact sheets, books, information, videos and DVDs on all aspects of ferrets and ferreting.

Further information can be obtained from the National Ferret School, Honeybank, Holestone Gate Road, Holestone Moor, Ashover, Derbyshire S45 0JS; telephone 01246 591590.

E-mail – info@ferret-school.co.uk. If requesting information via the postal service, please enclose a large (A4) sae, with suitable stamp attached.

More details are available via our web site – www.ferret-school.co.uk

TECHNICAL TERMS

Falconry has a language of its own, and there are many technical terms used by falconers throughout the world. Throughout this book, I have attempted to explain such technical terms as and when they have been used.

Sadly, as with all languages, some of the words and terms become out of date, unfashionable or simply unused. The following gives details of some of the more commonly used terms, words and expressions in use in modern day falconry.

ACCIPITER	-	A shortwinged or 'true' hawk, e.g. sparrowhawk, goshawk.
AUSTRINGER	-	A falconer who only flies short- or broadwinged hawks.
AYLMERI	-	Leather bands fitted around the hawk's feet, and used for tethering the hawk.
BATE	-	When a hawk attempts to fly from the fist or block when tethered, or flings itself away from the falconer.
BEWIT	-	A strip of leather used to attach items to the hawk, e.g. bell.
BIND	-	To grab and hold quarry.
BLAIN	-	An afflication of a hawk's joints similar to tennis elbow or housemaid's knee.
BLAST FREEZING	-	Rapid freezing of freshly killed animals to ensure freshness and nutritional value are maintained.
BLEEPER	-	A ferret finder, i.e. telemetry for use on ferrets.
BLOCK	-	A perch, usually rounded; also a generic term for any perch given to a hawk.
BLOCKED	-	A hawk placed on a perch (whether a bow or block perch) is said to be blocked.
BOW (PERCH)	-	A perch shaped like a bow.
BOWSER	-	A hawk which drinks more than normal.
BRANCHER	-	A young hawk having just left the nest.
BROADWING	-	A buzzard or eagle; also the Harris' hawk.
BROODER	-	A heated enclosure used to keep very young hawks warm.
BUMBLEFOOT	-	The generic term for infection/inflammation of a hawk's foot/feet.
CADGE	-	A device on which hawks are tethered and carried.
CALL OFF	-	To signal the hawk to leave its perching place and return to the falconer.

CARRY	-	When a hawk takes its newly caught prey and carries it away from the falconer, to a place where it can be eaten. An extremely undesirable vice in any hawk.
CAST	-	i To hold down a hawk when carrying out maintenance work on it. ii Fibre/roughage given to a hawk in the form of fur or feather. iii The act of a hawk bringing up undigested material. iv The pellet brought up by the hawk when it casts. v Two hawks flown together.
CASTING	-	Fibre or roughage given as part of the hawk's feed, i.e. fur or feather on the food.
CERE	-	The flesh/skin on the top of a hawk's beak.
CONDITION	-	The weight of a hawk: when too heavy, it is said to be in high condition, too light in low condition, and just right, it is said to be at flying weight.
COPE	-	To trim the hawk's beak and/or talons.
COURT	-	An aviary-like structure used to house ferrets.
CUB	-	The correct term for a hutch in which ferrets are kept.
CRAB	-	The seizing of a hawk by another. This is usually, though not always, when the hawks are tethered too close to each other, and the hawk strikes sideways to grab the other hawk.
CREANCE	-	A long length of string or nylon twine (approximately 30 metres/100 feet), used when training the hawk.
DECK FEATHERS	-	The central two feathers in the hawk's train/tail.
DUMMY BUNNY	-	An imitation rabbit used to train a hawk to chase/catch real rabbits.
ENTER	-	To allow a hawk to kill its first quarry.
EYAS	-	A young hawk.
FALCONER	-	One who trains and flies birds of prey to catch live quarry.
FEAK	-	The action of a hawk wiping its beak after feeding.
FED UP	-	A hawk which has eaten its full feed for the day.
FEED UP	-	To give a hawk its full feed for the day.
FERRET FINDER	-	Telemetry used on ferrets, to aid their recovery from rabbit warrens.
FLYING WEIGHT	-	The ideal weight at which a hawk can be flown at quarry, and still respond to the falconer.
FOOT	-	When a hawk grabs with its foot – it may foot quarry or even a human hand.
FRET MARKS OR LINES	-	The marks on feathers caused by undernourishment of the hawk while the feathers are growing.
FROUNCE	-	Avian trichomoniasis.
FURNITURE	-	Any item fitted to a hawk.

GORGE	-	To allow the hawk to eat as much as it wants at one single feed; an alternative name for the hawk's crop.
GRAFT	-	A spade used to dig out ferrets from rabbit warrens.
HARD DOWN	-	Feathers which have fully and completely grown.
HARD PENNED	-	As above.
HIGH	-	Relates to the weight of a hawk; high signifies heavy.
HOB	-	A male ferret.
HOBLET	-	A vasectomised male ferret.
IMP	-	To repair a damaged/broken feather by using a pin to affix another.
IMPRINT	-	A hawk reared by human hand.
IN BLOOD	-	Feathers which have not fully grown. At this stage, the feathers still retain their blood supply and, if damaged, will bleed and may never grow properly.
JESSES	-	Straps made from leather or nylon used in conjunction with a swivel and a leash to tether a hawk.
JILL	-	A female ferret.
JILL-JAB	-	A hormone injection used to take a female ferret out of oestrus.
KIT	-	A young (under 16 weeks old) ferret.
LAID-UP	-	A ferret which, for any of several reasons, has stayed underground while hunting.
LED	-	A light-emitting diode, a low current electric light.
LEASH	-	A length of nylon rope, with a knot at one end used, in conjunction with a swivel and jesses, to tether a hawk.
LONGWING	-	A falcon.
LOW	-	Relates to the weight of a hawk; low signifies underweight.
MAKE IN	-	To move – slowly and keeping low – towards a hawk on a kill or a lure.
MAKING TO THE HOOD	-	Accustoming a hawk to accept a hood.
MANNING	-	Habituating a hawk to the actions of humans.
MANTLE	-	When a hawk covers its food with its wings, in order to prevent other hawks from seeing and therefore stealing the food.
MEWS	-	Traditional building where hawks were kept to moult, but now used for a building where hawks are kept at night or in poor weather.
MUSKET	-	Male sparrowhawk.
MUTES	-	Hawk faeces.
PANCYTOPAENIA	-	Abnormal depression of all three cell types of the blood – a potentially fatal condition in female ferrets, caused by the females being left in oestrus.
PICK-UP PIECE	-	A small piece of meat used to tempt a hawk to jump onto the falconer's gloved fist.

PIP	-	The action of a chick in the egg beginning to break out.
PITCH	-	i To land.
		ii The height and position at which a hawk will wait on.
PUT IN	-	i To drive quarry into cover.
		ii When a hawk throws itself into cover in pursuit of its quarry.
PUT OVER	-	When a hawk empties its crop and swallows the contents.
RANGLE	-	Small pebbles given to a hawk to swallow and which help improve the hawk's condition.
RAPTOR	-	A bird of prey or owl, from the Latin *rapio*, meaning – '*to seize, snatch, to tear away*'.
ROUSE	-	The action of a hawk when it raises its feathers and shakes to remove surface dust, water etc.
SAILS	-	A hawk's wings.
SERVE	-	To flush quarry for a hawk; to present a lure for the hawk.
SHARP	-	Keen and in hunting condition; originally used only for longwings, but today is applied to any hawk.
SHARP SET	-	As above.
SHORTWING	-	A 'true' hawk, an accipiter, e.g. sparrowhawk, goshawk.
SLICING	-	The expulsion of excrement by a hawk.
SLIP	-	To release a hawk with the intention of it chasing quarry.
STRIKE	-	When a hawk hits its quarry.
STRIKE THE HOOD	-	Remove the hood from a hawk.
STOOP	-	The headlong dive of a longwing (falcon).
SWIVEL	-	A metal device used to connect the hawk's leash to its jesses.
TAKE STAND	-	When a hawk sits in a tree, usually when hunting ground game, e.g. rabbits.
TELEMETRY	-	Electronic radio tracking equipment, essential for locating a missing hawk.
THROW UP	-	When a hawk mounts steeply, usually after a stoop.
TIERCEL	-	Traditionally the term for the male peregrine, but today used for the male of any species of hawk.
TIRING	-	A tough piece of meat, with little nutritional value, given to a hawk to give it work, relieve boredom, strengthen neck muscles etc., e.g. a rabbit head or foot.
TRAIN	-	A hawk's tail.
TRANSPONDER	-	A transmitter. Those used for hawks are radio transmitters while those used for ferrets may use electro-magnetism.
WAIT ON	-	When a longwing waits above the falconer and his dog, waiting for the quarry to be flushed.
WEATHER	-	Placing a hawk on open ground for it to take the weather.
YAGI	-	The directional aerial attached to the receiver for use with a hawk's telemetry.
YARAK	-	An Arab expression meaning a hawk in 100% hunting condition.

USEFUL ORGANISATIONS

THE NATIONAL FALCONRY SCHOOL

Holestone Gate Road
Holestone Moor
Ashover
Derbyshire S45 0JS
Tel: 01246 591590
www.falconry-school.co.uk
info@falconry-school.co.uk

The author's falconry school which runs courses on all aspects of falconry, as well as specialist courses for veterinary professionals, police officers and other professionals involved with raptors.

The School also runs activity events for members of the public, team-building events, photographic days and instructional courses and provides corporate entertainment services.

The School can supply hawks, owls, falcons, equipment, DVDs, books, etc. on all aspects of falconry.

The School has over fifty raptors and supplies many of them to TV and film makers as avian animal actors.

The School also takes in and rehabilitates injured wild raptors.

The School is a Lantra Approved Training Centre.

THE NATIONAL FERRET SCHOOL

Holestone Gate Road
Holestone Moor
Ashover
Derbyshire S45 0JS
Tel: 01246 591590
www.ferret-school.co.uk
info@ferret-school.co.uk

Working very closely with the National Falconry School, the National Ferret School runs courses and events on all aspects of ferrets and ferreting, and can supply ferrets, equipment, DVDs, books, etc. on the subjects.

The National Ferret School holds a database of 'ferret friendly vets' and publishes information sheets on all aspects of ferret care.

THE INDEPENDENT BIRD REGISTER (IBR)

Tiercel House
Falcon Close
Scotton
North Yorkshire DL9 3RB
Tel: 01748 830112
www.ibr.org.uk
juliana@ibr.org.uk

The IBR offers a registration scheme, and registers raptors and their owners on its database. When a hawk is reported lost or found to the IBR, all efforts are made to reunite hawk and owner as soon as possible. The IBR maintains a constant liaison with police, Defra, RSPCA and falconers. The organisation also issues closed rings for use on raptors.

THE HAWK BOARD

Mike Clowes,
Le Moulin de l`Age
86390 Lathus St Remy
France
Tel: 0033 54991 7930 0033
www.hawkboard-cff.org.uk
michael.clowes@orange.fr

The Hawk Board represents UK falconers and raptor keepers, and is the first point of contact between raptor keepers and government departments. It is included in any consultation on new laws or changes to existing legislation concerning falconry and the keeping and breeding of raptors.

THE CAMPAIGN FOR FALCONRY

Doreen Page
Tel: 01933 665800
doreen.page@btinternet.com

The Campaign for Falconry was formed in 1997 as an initiative between The Hawk Board and the Countryside Alliance. Its *raison d'être* is to raise funds and awareness to defend falconry and raptor keeping in the UK.

CROWN FALCONRY

48 Kent Street
Hasland
Chesterfield
Derbyshire S41 0PL
www.crownfalconry.co.uk

Manufacturers and suppliers of top quality falconry furniture, perches, gloves etc.

BRITISH ASSOCIATION FOR SHOOTING & CONSERVATION (BASC)

UK Headquarters
Marford Mill
Rossett
Wrexham
Clwyd LL12 0HL
Tel: 01244 573000
www.basc.org.uk

The BASC is the UK's largest country sports organisation, and represents its members while involved in any legitimate and legal country sport. Membership of the Association confers excellent insurance cover while the member is involved in any legal country sport.

THE COUNTRYSIDE ALLIANCE (CA)

The Old Town Hall
367 Kennington Road
London SE11 4PT
Tel: 020 7840 9200
www.countryside-alliance.org.uk

The CA campaigns on a wide range of countryside and rural issues, and membership includes insurance cover while participating in legal country sports.

DEPARTMENT FOR ENVIRONMENT, FOOD & RURAL AFFAIRS (Defra)

Customer Contact Unit
Eastbury House
30–34 Albert Embankment
London SE1 7TL
Tel 08459 335577
www.defra.gov.uk
helpline@defra.gsi.gov.uk

The UK Government department tasked with issues such as the environment, rural development, the countryside, wildlife, animal welfare and similar issues.

LANTRA AWARDS

Lantra House
Stoneleigh Park
nr Coventry
Warwickshire CV8 2LG
Tel: 024 7641 9703
Fax: 024 7641 1655
awards@lantra-awards.co.uk

Lantra is a UK training organisation, specialising in land-based industries. Working with professional falconers throughout the UK, a new award 'Beginning Falconry' was formulated and introduced, and is now offered at many 'Lantra Approved Training Centres' throughout the UK. 'Beginning Falconry' is a formal award intended for those new to the sport, or those who wish to keep raptors. Approved by the UK's Hawk Board, while administered by Lantra Awards, the award assumes that candidates have no previous knowledge or experience of falconry and covers all aspects of management and husbandry of birds of prey up to flying a raptor to the fist on a creance.

It is hoped that there will be further awards – covering advanced husbandry, breeding and falconry practices – thereby providing a progressive path for candidates.

The National Falconry School delivers the 'Beginning Falconry' Award.

Structure of the Award
The Award is divided into two Units:

Unit 1 Bird of Prey Management and Husbandry
* Module 1 – Housing
* Module 2 – Hygiene
* Module 3 – Feeding and Food Preparation
* Module 4 – Health
* Module 5 – Species Suitability
* Module 6 – Purchasing Your First Bird

Unit 2 Falconry Basics
* Module 7 – Essential Equipment
* Module 8 – Picking Up and Carrying
* Module 9 – Feeding, Manning and Initial Training Techniques
* Module 10 – Weighing and Weight Management
* Module 11 – Flying to the Fist on a Creance

Although intended for the newcomer to the sport, the award can also be achieved by practising falconers.

Full details of the Lantra Beginning Falconry Course can be obtained from Lantra (details above) or The National Falconry School, a Lantra Approved Centre info@falconry-school.co.uk

BIBLIOGRAPHY

Beebe, Frank L., *The Compleat Falconer,* Hancock House, 1992.

Beebe, Frank L., *A Falconry Manual,* Hancock House, 1992.

Beynon, Peter H. (ed), *Manual of Raptors, Pigeons and Waterfowl,* British Small Animal Veterinary Association, 1996.

Brown, Leslie & Amadon, Dean, *Eagles, Hawks & Falcons of the World,* Wellfleet, 1989.

Cooper, John E., *Veterinary Aspects of Captive Birds of Prey,* Standfast Press, 1978, 1985.

Drummond, Humphrey, *Falconry for You,* John Gifford, 1983.

Durman-Walters, Diana, *The Modern Falconer,* Swan Hill Press, 1994.

Ford, Emma, *Falconry Art and Practice,* Cassell, 1992.

Ford, Emma, *Birds of Prey,* Batsford, 1982.

Ford, Emma, *Falconry,* Shire Publications, 1998.

Ford, Emma, *Falconry in Mews and Field,* Batsford, 1982.

Ford, Emma, *Gyrfalcon,* John Murray, 1999.

Ford, Emma, *Peregrine,* Fourth Estate, 1993.

Fox, Nick, *Understanding the Bird of Prey,* Hancock House, 1995.

Glasier, Phillip, *Falconry and Hawking,* Batsford, 1978.

Hollinshead, Martin, *The Complete Rabbit & Hare Book,* The Fernhill Press, 1999.

Hollinshead, Martin, *Hawking with Golden Eagles,* The Fernhill Press, 1995.

Hollinshead, Martin, *Hawking Ground Quarry,* The Fernhill Press, 1993.

Hollinshead, Martin, *A Mixed Bag,* The Fernhill Press, 2004.

Hollinshead, Martin, *A Passion for Harris' Hawks,* The Fernhill Press, 2002.

Illingworth, Frank, *Falcons & Falconry,* Blandford, 1975.

McKay, James, *The Complete Guide to Ferrets,* Swan Hill Press, 2002.

McKay, James, *Ferret Breeding,* Swan Hill Press, 2006.

McKay, James, *The Ferret and Ferreting Handbook,* The Crowood Press, 1989.

Mavrogordato, Jack, *A Hawk for the Bush,* Neville Spearman, 1960.

Salvin, F. H. and Brodrick, W., *Falconry in the British Isles (1855),* Beech Publishing, 1997.

Upton, Roger, *Falconry Principle & Practice,* A & C Black, 1991.

Upton, Roger, *Hood, Leash and Lure,* RC & J Upton, 2004.

Upton, Roger, *O for a Falconer's Voice,* The Crowood Press, 1987.

Walker, Adrian, *The Encyclopaedia of Falconry,* Swan Hill Press, 1999.

Weaver, James D & Cade, Tom J, Editors, *Falcon Propagation – A Manual on captive Breeding* The Peregrine Fund, Inc., 1985

Woodford, M. H., *A Manual of Falconry,* A & C Black, 1960.

INDEX